★★★ AMERICA'S FAVORITE
BEEF RECIPES

★ GREAT HOME COOKING FROM COAST TO COAST ★

The National Cattlemen's Beef Association

Concept Development/Editorial Direction
Food Communications Department

Recipe Development
The Beef & Veal Culinary Center

Photographer
Hans Rott

Food Stylists
Lois Hlavac, Judy Vance

Prop Stylists
Nancy Wall Hopkins, Karen Johnson

Copy Writing/Editorial Assistance
McDowell & Piasecki Food Communications, Inc.

Nutritional Analysis
Patricia Godfrey, R.D., Nutrition & Food Associates, Inc.

First printing. Printed in U.S.A.
Pre-Press Services, Time-Life Imaging Center

Time-Life Books is a division of Time Life Inc.

Time Life Inc.

PRESIDENT AND CEO
George Artandi

Time-Life Books

PRESIDENT
Stephen R. Frary

Time-Life Custom Publishing

VICE PRESIDENT AND PUBLISHER
Terry Newell

Vice President of Sales and Marketing
Neil Levin

Editor
Linda Bellamy

Director of Design
Christopher M. Register

Production Manager
Carolyn Clark

Quality Assurance Manager
James D. King

TIME-LIFE is a trademark of Time Warner Inc. U.S.A.

Library of Congress Cataloging-in-Publication Data

America's favorite beef recipes: great home cooking
from coast to coast.
     p. cm.
    Includes index.
    ISBN 0-7370-0004-X
    1. Cookery (Beef) 2. Cookery, American.
    3. Quick and easy cookery.
TX749.5.B43A45 1998
641.6'62—dc21
                  98-16649
                  CIP

Books produced by Time-Life Custom Publishing are
available at a special bulk discount for promotional
and premium use. Custom adaptations can also be
created to meet your specific marketing goals.
Call 1-800-323-5255.

★ ★ ★ **AMERICA'S FAVORITE**

BEEF RECIPES

America's Favorite Beef Recipes

★ Beef is an American favorite—it's consumed 76 million times each day across America. In fact beef has a larger share of supermarket sales than fresh poultry, pork and seafood combined. ★ We love beef for its great taste; it satisfies our desire for bold, flavorful food. Plus, beef is very easy to prepare and it's versatile. There's a choice for any occasion and every budget. This collection of recipes has been created with beef lovers—and today's cook—in mind. ★ Delicious favorites—both classic and contemporary recipes—bring out the best of beef. All 77 recipes promise a great beef eating experience every time you prepare and serve them. ★ Six enticing recipe chapters offer convenient, delicious meal solutions for every occasion from easy meals for the family to company-perfect dinners, for casual entertaining, grilling, even bonus meals, where you cook once and have the makings for two meals. ★ Most of these recipes are prepared with eight ingredients or less (excluding salt, ground black pepper and water) and are ready in under an hour. More than half can be on the table in 30 minutes or less. ★

Other special features in this book:

★ *Streamlined, step-by-step recipes that have been Triple Tested in the Beef & Veal Culinary Center ensuring that the novice or experienced cook can easily prepare them with outstanding results.*

★ *Recipes prepared with ingredients that are easy to find in the supermarket.*

★ *Recipes made with basic cooking utensils and equipment that are found in most kitchens.*

★ *Nutritional information for each recipe so that you can determine the calories, protein, carbohydrate, fat, iron, sodium and cholesterol in a serving of the recipe. See pages 136-139.*

★ *Helpful cooking tips.*

★ *39 beef recipes that can be prepared and served in 30 minutes or less. They will be identified by this symbol:* ⊖

★ *Everything you need to know about purchasing beef at the supermarket and storing beef at home.*

★ *1-2-3 easy steps to each cooking method used in the recipes including pan-broiling, broiling, pan-frying, stir-frying, roasting, grilling, cooking in liquid and braising.*

★ *A helpful guide to determining the doneness of beef.*

All of these special features add up to a great beef eating experience, so go ahead and enjoy preparing these easy, versatile, delicious beef recipes. There's something to please every beef lover!

Inspection Stamp

Grading Stamps

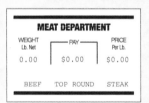

Retail Label

Buying Beef

With more than 60 different beef cuts available in the meat case, questions some-times arise. How do you know which cut to select? How do you know the beef will be fresh, high quality, good tasting and safe?

Meat Inspection

First, the wholesomeness of our meat supply is ensured by meat inspection conducted by the U.S. Department of Agriculture (USDA). All meat that is sold must, by law, pass inspection. Inspection provides assurance that all meat sold is wholesome and accurately labeled. U.S. meat products have a safety record that is envied throughout the world, thanks to the thorough inspection process. Meat inspection, paid by tax funds, is not synonymous with meat grading.

Beef Grading

Beef grading is optional and is paid for by meat packers and processors and ultimately by the consumer in the price of beef. Beef is graded for quality by USDA graders according to standards established by the USDA. Beef quality grades indicate palatability. While there are eight quality grades for beef, the three frequently found at retail are **Prime, Choice** and **Select.**

Young beef with the most marbling is given the Prime or highest quality grade. Prime is usually sold to restaurants, but may be available in some specialty markets. Choice is the most widely available grade in the retail market. Select has the least amount of marbling, but may not be as tender, juicy or flavorful as Prime or Choice.

Labeling

The meat package label identifies the kind of beef, the primal (wholesale) cut and the retail cut name. It also states the weight, price per pound and total price of the beef item. It may include a grade, a sell-by date, a UPC bar or even preparation/cooking information. On ground beef labels you should also look for an indication of the leanness or composition — either % lean, % fat or both.

How Much To Buy?

The amount of beef you need to buy varies with the cut selected. Refer to the following chart for helpful guidelines.

Beef Cut	Servings Per Pound *
Steaks	
Chuck Shoulder, boneless	3 1/2
Chuck Top Blade, boneless	3
Flank	4
Porterhouse/T-Bone	2 1/2
Rib	2 1/2
Ribeye	3
Tenderloin	4
Top Loin, boneless	3 3/4
Top Round	4
Top Sirloin, boneless	3 1/2
Round Tip	4
Pot Roasts	
Chuck Arm, boneless	2 1/2 to 3
Chuck Blade, boneless	3
Chuck Shoulder, boneless	3
Brisket	2 1/2 to 3

Beef Cut	Servings Per Pound *
Roasts	
Eye Round	4
Ribeye	3 to 3 1/2
Rib	2 1/2
Round Tip	3 1/2 to 4
Tri-Tip	4
Other Cuts	
Beef for Stew	2 1/2 to 3
Ground Beef	4
Shank Cross Cuts	1 1/2 to 2 1/2
Short Ribs	1 1/2 to 2 1/2
Short Ribs, boneless	2 1/2 to 3

* Based on 3-ounce cooked, trimmed servings.

What To Look For At The Store

★ *Choose beef with a bright cherry-red color, without any grayish or brown blotches. The exception is vacuum-packaged beef, which, due to a lack of oxygen, has a darker purplish-red color. When exposed to the air, it will turn to a bright red.*

★ *Look for beef that is firm to the touch, not soft.*

★ *Make sure the package is cold and has no holes or tears. Excessive liquid in a package may indicate improper storage or beef that is past its optimum shelf life.*

★ *For highest quality, purchase beef before the sell-by date.*

★ *Select beef just before checking out. If it will take longer than 30 minutes to get home, keep beef cold in a cooler until it can be refrigerated.*

Beef Storage

★ **Refrigerator Storage (35° to 40°F)**

Fresh Beef

Steaks, Roasts	3 to 4 days
Beef for Stew	2 to 3 days
Ground Beef	1 to 2 days
Cooked Beef	3 to 4 days

★ **Freezer Storage (0°F or colder)**

Fresh Beef

Steaks, Roasts	6 to 12 months
Beef for Stew	6 to 12 months
Ground Beef	3 to 4 months
Cooked Beef	2 to 3 months

In The Refrigerator

Select beef last when shopping to ensure that it stays as cold as possible. Choose packages that are cold and tightly wrapped without tears or punctures.

Upon arriving home, immediately place beef in the refrigerator meat compartment or coldest part of the refrigerator. Beef wrapped in transparent film requires no additional wrapping. However, you may want to place it on a tray or in a plastic bag, in case the original packaging leaks.

In The Freezer

Immediately freeze any beef you don't plan to use within a few days and store it at 0°F or colder. Label each package with the date, name of beef cut and weight or number of servings.

Beef can be frozen in its original transparent packaging for up to 2 weeks. For longer storage, prevent freezer burn by rewrapping the beef in moisture-proof airtight material such as freezer paper or heavy-duty aluminum foil, or place in a food-safe plastic freezer bag. *Press out as much air as possible before sealing.*

To defrost beef safely, place in the refrigerator on a tray to catch any juices. Defrost large roasts for 4 to 7 hours per pound; smaller roasts for 3 to 5 hours per pound; and ground beef for 24 hours for a 1 to 1½-inch-thick package. *For food safety reasons, never defrost beef at room temperature.*

Beef And Health

Balance, variety and moderation are still the keys to healthful eating. The 1995 Dietary Guidelines for Americans emphasize that no one food provides all of the nutrients needed for good health; eating a variety of foods is the best way to ensure that you get the energy, protein, vitamins, minerals and fiber that you need.

The USDA Food Guide Pyramid illustrates what foods need to be consumed each day: 2 to 3 servings from the Meat Group (or a total of 5 to 7 ounces each day); 2 to 3 servings from the Milk, Yogurt & Cheese Group; 3 to 5 servings from the Vegetable Group; 2 to 4 servings from the Fruit Group; and 6 to 11 servings from the Bread, Cereal, Rice & Pasta Group.

In addition, the Dietary Guidelines recommend consuming less than 300 mg of cholesterol daily. They also recommend that less than 30 percent of our total caloric intake comes from fat (with less than 10 percent from saturated fatty acids, less than 10 percent from polyunsaturated fatty acids and less than 10 percent from monounsaturated fatty acids). In evaluating the fat content of your diet, it's not necessary to balance every meal precisely. In fact, look at meals over a few days, even over the course of a week. It's balance over time, not just for one day, that counts.

Beef easily fits within the guidelines for healthful eating. Beef provides high-quality protein, complete with all eight essential amino acids. It is also one of the most important sources of dietary iron and zinc. And beef contains significant amounts of the B-complex vitamins riboflavin, niacin, thiamin, B_6 and B_{12} essential for good health.

Today's beef is leaner than it used to be. The average thickness of fat around the edge of steaks and roasts is less than $1/8$ inch, with over 40 percent of cuts having no external fat at all. When choosing a lean cut of beef, look for "loin" or "round" in the name (i.e., sirloin, top round); these are the leanest.

A great way to visualize a serving of beef is to think of a deck of playing cards. A 3-ounce cooked, trimmed portion is about the same size as a standard deck of cards.★

★ A standard deck of cards measures $2^1/4$ x $3^1/4$ x $5/8$ inches.

Cooking Beef

The Most Popular Steaks Purchased At Retail
(based on pounds)

1 Sirloin

2 Round

3 Chuck

4 Porterhouse/T-Bone

5 Rib

6 Cubed

7 Flank

8 Tenderloin

Source: NPD/MPD, NCBA, 1996

What's the secret to successfully cooking beef so that it's tender, juicy and flavorful? It's easy. Choose the correct cooking method. The cooking method is determined by the beef cut and whether it is a tender or less tender cut.

Two factors help determine the tenderness of beef cuts.

★ *One is the amount of connective tissue. Cuts with more connective tissue are less tender than those with smaller amounts of it.*

★ *Also, the location of the cut affects tenderness. Beef cuts from the center of the animal (the loin and rib) are suspension muscles. They receive little or no exercise so they're tender. Cuts from the front and rear of the animal (the chuck and round) are more heavily exercised and are less tender.*

Cooking Methods

Dry heat cooking methods such as pan-broiling, broiling, pan-frying, stir-frying, roasting and grilling are generally used to cook tender beef cuts. Beef cooks quickly over medium to medium-high heat. *Moist* heat cooking methods (also called braising, cooking in liquid, simmering and stewing) are used to cook less tender cuts. Adding liquid and simmering gently in a tightly covered pan develop the flavor of less tender cuts and ensure that they are fork-tender.

Some less tender beef cuts (such as chuck shoulder steak, top round steak, eye round steak and flank steak) can be cooked by dry heat if marinated first in a mixture containing an acidic ingredient such as lemon juice, yogurt, wine or vinegar or a natural tenderizing enzyme found in fresh papaya, ginger, pineapple and figs.

Cooking Methods

Beef Cut	Pan-broil	Pan-fry	Stir-fry	Broil	Roast	Grill	Cooking in Liquid	Braise
Chuck								
Chuck Top Blade Steak, *boneless*	●	●	●	●		●		●
Chuck Shoulder Steak, *boneless*	▲	▲		▲		▲		●
Chuck Eye Steak, *boneless*	●	●	●	●		●		●
Chuck Pot Roast (*Arm, Blade, Shoulder*)							●	●
Short Ribs							●	●
Rib								
Ribeye Steak	●	●	●	●		●		
Rib Roast, Ribeye Roast					●	●		
Short Loin								
Porterhouse/T-Bone Steak	●	●		●		●		
Tenderloin Steak, Top Loin Steak	●	●	●	●		●		
Tenderloin Roast					●	●		
Sirloin								
Sirloin Steak, Top Sirloin Steak, *boneless*	●	●	●	●		●		
Round								
Round Tip Steak, *thin cut*	●	●	●					
Round Steak							●	●
Top Round Steak	■	■	●	■		■	●	
Other Cuts								
Brisket, *Fresh or Corned*							●	●
Flank Steak			●	▲		▲		●
Cubed Steak	●	●	●					●
Ground Beef	●	●	●	●	●	●		
Beef for Stew							●	●

Key

▲ *Marinate 30 minutes to 6 hours before cooking*

■ *Marinate 6 to 8 hours or overnight before cooking*

DELICIOUS

EASY!

Cooking Beef... 1-2-3 Easy

Dry or moist heat cookery methods are 1-2-3 EASY!

Dry Heat Methods

★ Pan-broiling ★

1 Heat heavy nonstick skillet over medium heat until hot.

2 Season beef (straight from refrigerator) with herbs or spices, if desired. Place beef in preheated skillet (do not overcrowd). Do not add oil or water. Do not cover.

3 Pan-broil according to recipe; turn once. (For cuts 1 inch thick, turn occasionally.) Remove excess drippings from skillet as they accumulate. After cooking, season beef with salt, if desired.

★ Broiling ★

1 Set oven to broil; preheat for 10 minutes. During broiling, the oven door for electric ranges should be left ajar; the oven door for gas ranges should remain closed. (However, consult the owner's manual for specific broiling guidelines.)

2 Place beef (straight from refrigerator) on rack of broiler pan. Season beef with herbs or spices, if desired. Position broiler pan so that surface of beef is within specified distance from the heat as indicated in recipe.

3 Broil according to recipe; turn once. After cooking, season beef with salt, if desired.

★ Pan-frying ★

1 Heat small amount of oil in heavy nonstick skillet over medium heat until hot.

2 Season beef (straight from refrigerator) with herbs or spices, if desired. Place beef in preheated skillet (do not overcrowd). Do not add water. Do not cover.

3 Pan-fry to desired doneness; turn occasionally. After cooking, season beef with salt, if desired.

★ Stir-frying (a variation of pan-frying) ★

1 Partially freeze beef for easier slicing, if desired. Cut into thin, uniform strips or pieces. Marinate to add flavor or tenderize while preparing other ingredients, if desired.

2 Heat small amount of oil in wok or large heavy nonstick skillet over medium-high heat until hot.

3 Stir-fry beef in half-pound batches (do not overcrowd), continuously turning with a scooping motion, until outside surface of beef is no longer pink. Add additional oil for each batch, if necessary. Cook beef and vegetables separately, then combine and heat through. The cooking liquid may be thickened with cornstarch dissolved in water, if desired.

★ Roasting ★

1 Heat oven to temperature as specified in recipe.

2 Place roast (straight from refrigerator), fat side up, on rack in shallow roasting pan. Season roast with herbs or spices, if desired. Insert ovenproof meat thermometer so tip is centered in thickest part of roast, not resting in fat or touching bone. Do not add water. Do not cover.

3 Roast according to recipe. Transfer roast to carving board; tent loosely with aluminum foil. Let roast stand 15 minutes. (Temperature will continue to rise 5°F to 10°F to reach desired doneness and roast will be easier to carve.)

★ Grilling ★

1 Prepare charcoal for grilling. When coals are medium, ash-covered (approximately 30 minutes), spread in single layer and check cooking temperature. Position cooking grid. (To check temperature, cautiously hold the palm of your hand above the coals at cooking height. Count the number of seconds you can hold your hand in that position before the heat forces you to pull it away; approximately 4 seconds for medium heat.)

EASY!

Continued on page 14

EASY!

2 Season beef (straight from refrigerator) with herbs or spices, if desired. Place on cooking grid directly over coals.

3 Grill according to recipe; turn occasionally. After cooking, season beef with salt, if desired.

(Note: gas grill brands vary greatly; for best results, consult your owner's manual for grilling guidelines.)

Moist Heat Methods

★ *Cooking in Liquid (also called stewing)* ★

1 Coat beef lightly with seasoned flour, if desired. Slowly brown beef on all sides in small amount of oil in heavy pan. Pour off drippings.

2 Cover beef with liquid (e.g., broth, water, juice, beer or wine). Add seasoning, if desired. Bring liquid to a boil; reduce heat to low.

3 Cover tightly and simmer gently over low heat on top of the range according to recipe or until beef is fork-tender. The cooking liquid may be reduced or thickened for a sauce, if desired.

★ *Braising (also called pot roasting)* ★

1 Slowly brown beef on all sides in small amount of oil in heavy pan. Pour off drippings. Season beef, if desired.

2 Add small amount (½ to 2 cups) of liquid (e.g., broth, water, juice, beer or wine).

3 Cover tightly and simmer gently over low heat on top of the range or in a 325°F oven according to recipe or until beef is fork-tender. The cooking liquid may be reduced or thickened for a sauce, if desired.

Marinades & Rubs

Marinades are seasoned liquid mixtures that add flavor and in some cases tenderize beef. A tenderizing marinade must contain an acidic ingredient such as lemon juice, yogurt, wine or vinegar, or a natural tenderizing enzyme found in fresh papaya, ginger, pineapple and figs.

A rub is a blend of seasonings, such as fresh or dried herbs and spices, applied to the surface of uncooked beef steaks, roasts or ground beef patties for flavor. Paste-type rubs often contain some oil, crushed garlic or mustard.

Follow these tips for successful marinating.

* ★ *Always marinate in the refrigerator, never at room temperature.*

* ★ *Tender beef cuts need to be marinated only 15 minutes or up to 2 hours to impart the flavor of the marinade.*

* ★ *Less tender beef cuts should be marinated at least 6 hours or up to 24 hours (unless recipe specifies otherwise) in a mixture containing a food acid or enzyme.*

* ★ *A tenderizing marinade penetrates about 1/4 inch into the surface of the beef.*

* ★ *Marinating longer than 24 hours in a tenderizing marinade can result in a mushy surface texture.*

* ★ *Never save and reuse a marinade.*

* ★ *Allow 1/4 to 1/2 cup marinade for each 1 to 2 pounds of beef.*

* ★ *Marinate in a food-safe plastic bag or nonreactive container. Turn or stir the beef occasionally to allow even exposure to the marinade.*

* ★ *If a marinade that has been in contact with uncooked meat is used for a sauce, bring it to a full rolling boil and boil for at least 1 minute before serving.*

Determining Doneness

Beef Steaks And Roasts Doneness Guide

MEDIUM RARE
Internal Temperature 145°F

MEDIUM
Internal Temperature 160°F

WELL DONE
Internal Temperature 170°F

To assure a great beef eating experience it's important to use the correct cooking method, but equally important is knowing when the beef is cooked to the proper doneness.

For Dry Heat

For beef cooked by dry heat methods, there are three ways to determine doneness: visually; internal temperature; and by touch.

Visually

Used most often for steaks or ground beef patties, simply cut a small slit using a sharp knife and check the color of the meat near the bone, or near the center of a boneless cut or patty. Ground beef patties should always be cooked to medium doneness (160°F) or until the center is no longer pink and juices show no pink color.

With A Thermometer

For roasts a thermometer is the best way to gauge internal temperature. There are several thermometer options available in addition to the traditional *ovenproof meat thermometer*, which is inserted into the beef and left there during the entire cooking process.

Instant-read thermometers are used toward the end of cooking time to check for doneness; the internal temperature registers in just a few seconds. They are not heatproof and cannot be left in the beef while it is being cooked.

The *thermometer/timer* features a base unit to which a long wire is connected; a temperature probe is connected to the other end of the wire. During cooking the base unit remains outside the oven or grill; the probe rests in the beef. A digital display on the base unit allows monitoring of the internal temperature during cooking.

By Touch

This method is used for steaks and takes the most practice. The touches for doneness are compared to how your skin feels at certain times. Here's how.

* *For Medium Rare: Make a loose fist with your hand. With the index finger of your other hand, touch the area between the thumb and index finger. The flesh will be springy with slight resistance but not hard. A medium rare steak should have a similar feeling when touched with your index finger.*

* *For Medium: Tightly clench your fist. Touch the same place again with the index finger of your other hand. It will feel firm, with minimal give. A steak cooked to medium doneness should have a similar feeling when touched with your index finger.*

For Moist Heat

Beef cooked by moist heat methods (cooking in liquid or braising) is always cooked well done. Beef should be cooked just until fork-tender and moist; a two-pronged utility fork can be easily inserted into the beef. Overcooking or cooking at too high temperature can result in dry, less flavorful beef.

Tips For Safe Cooking

Cooking Ground Beef

 The Beef & Veal Culinary Center recommends these guidelines for ground beef. For ½-inch-thick ground beef patties (4 ounces each), heat large non-stick skillet over medium heat until hot. Place patties, directly from refrigerator, in skillet. Cook 10 to 12 minutes to medium (160°F) doneness or until centers are no longer pink and juices show no pink color; turn once. For ground beef crumbles, cook and break up ground beef over medium heat until no pink remains and juices show no pink color. The cooking time can be shortened if the crumbles will continue to cook in a recipe; follow recipe directions carefully.

★ Defrost frozen homemade patties in the refrigerator prior to cooking. For purchased pre-formed frozen patties, follow package directions.

Food safety in the kitchen is everyone's responsibility. To help avoid cross-contamination and prevent foodborne illness, follow these easy steps.

★ *Wash hands thoroughly in hot soapy water before and after handling meat and other fresh foods.*

★ *Keep raw meat and meat juices from coming into contact with other foods during preparation.*

★ *Wash all utensils, cutting surfaces and counters with hot soapy water after contact with raw meat.*

★ *Keep carving boards separate from other cutting boards.*

★ *If a marinade is to be used for basting or as a sauce, reserve a portion of it before adding the beef. If a marinade that has been in contact with uncooked meat is used for a sauce, bring it to a full rolling boil and boil for at least 1 minute before serving.*

★ *Never save and reuse a marinade.*

What Is The Proper Doneness?

★ *The U.S. Department of Agriculture (USDA)/Food Safety and Inspection Service (FSIS) recommends cooking beef steaks and roasts to a minimum internal temperature of 145°F (medium rare). Cook ground beef patties to 160°F (medium).*

⊘ *For safety reasons, never eat raw or rare ground beef.*

Tips For Successful Cooking

Perfectly cooked beef is easy if you keep these guidelines in mind.

★ *Use the correct cooking temperatures specified in recipes.*

★ *High heat can overcook or char the outside of beef cuts while the inside remains underdone. To assure tender beef, you generally use medium heat with dry cookery methods and low heat for moist cookery methods.*

★ *Use an oven thermometer to check that your oven is accurate.*

★ *Cooking times in these recipes are based on beef taken directly from the refrigerator.*

★ *Cooking times for Select and Choice grades are comparable. However, for Select beef, be careful not to overcook as it can quickly become dry and less flavorful.*

★ *Because the round is very lean, purchase high-quality branded beef, or Prime or Choice grade for best results in recipes calling for round steak.*

★ *Cooking times for gas and electric ranges are comparable. However, since individual ranges perform differently, it's important that you become familiar with your own range.*

★ *Turn steaks and roasts with tongs. Do not use a fork, which pierces the beef and allows flavorful juices to escape.*

★ *Turn ground beef patties with a spatula. Do not flatten them; flavorful juices escape resulting in a dry burger.*

★ *Leave a thin layer of fat on steaks and roasts during cooking to preserve juiciness. Trim fat after cooking.*

Continued on page 20

Tips For Successful Cooking

Cookware Basics

★ **Weight**
Choose pans that are thick enough to heat evenly.

★ **Materials**
Copper and aluminum conduct heat readily and respond quickly to temperature changes.

Stainless steel is less conductive and can heat unevenly.

Cast iron, plain or enameled, is slow to heat up but holds the heat for a long time.

Glass conducts heat poorly.

★ **Surfaces**
Nonstick surfaces are easier to clean and they allow cooking with less fat.

Aluminum and cast iron are reactive metals; they can affect the taste and color of dishes that contain acidic ingredients. Use cookware with a nonreactive interior surface of anodized aluminum, stainless steel, enamel or nonstick.

What's The Right Equipment?

For best results, use the pan size specified in the recipe. A pan that is too small can cause crowding, which interferes with browning, or can result in spillovers. A pan that is too large can result in overcooking. If in doubt, refer to the following chart to select the correct size.

Skillet Size	Skillet Diameter
Small	*6 to 8 inches*
Medium	*8 to 10 inches*
Large	*10 to 12 inches*

Saucepan Size	Saucepan Volume
Small	*1 to 1½ quarts (4 to 6 cups)*
Medium	*2 quarts (8 cups)*
Large	*3 to 4 quarts (12 to 16 cups)*
Dutch Oven/ Stock Pot	*5 to 8 quarts (20 to 32 cups)*

Casserole Size	Baking Dish Substitution
1½ quart	*10 x 6 inch*
2 quart	*11 x 7 or 8-inch square*
2½ quart	*9-inch square*
3 quart	*13 x 9 inch*

Measuring — Another Key To Success

Correct measurements contribute to successful recipes. Follow these tips for success.

 Measure flour, sugar and other dry or solid ingredients in graduated measuring cups (usually metal or plastic cups in sets that include 1-cup, 1/2-cup, 1/3-cup and 1/4-cup measures) that can be filled to the top and leveled with a spatula or the flat side of a table knife. Don't shake or pack dry ingredients unless specified in the recipe (example: packed brown sugar should be pressed firmly into the cup).

 Measure liquid ingredients in clear glass (or plastic) measuring cups with a spout. Place cup on a level surface and add desired amount of liquid; read the measure at eye level.

Nutritional Analysis Information

The recipes in this book were analyzed by a registered dietitian following these parameters.

- ★ *If more than one ingredient was listed, the first option was used.*
- ★ *Optional ingredients and garnishes were not included.*
- ★ *The smallest number of servings was used when a range was listed.*
- ★ *The lowest amount of ingredients was used when a range was listed.*
- ★ *If the food was marinated, the estimated amount absorbed was included.*

See pages 136-139 for nutrition information.

Measuring Equivalents

Dash or pinch	*under 1/8 teaspoon*
1/2 tablespoon	*1 1/2 teaspoons*
1 tablespoon	*3 teaspoons*
1 ounce liquid	*2 tablespoons*
1/4 cup	*4 tablespoons*
1/3 cup	*5 tablespoons, plus 1 teaspoon*
1/2 cup	*8 tablespoons*
2/3 cup	*10 tablespoons, plus 2 teaspoons*
3/4 cup	*12 tablespoons*
1 cup	*16 tablespoons*
1 cup	*8 ounces*
1 pound	*16 ounces*

Kitchen Express

Chapter 1

These 20 minutes or less beef recipes get you in and out of the kitchen fast. Some make great family meals, others are appropriate for entertaining. From soups, sandwiches and salads to wraps and pockets, all are bursting with flavor and guaranteed to become new mainstays in your quick-cook repertoire.

15-Minute Pot Roast With Savory Potatoes, Page 31

Pesto Beef Sandwich-In-The-Round

1 ¼ pounds thinly sliced deli roast beef

1 round loaf crusty French *or* Italian bread (10 to 12-inch diameter)

⅓ cup light mayonnaise

3 tablespoons prepared basil pesto sauce

1 teaspoon fresh lemon juice

1 jar (7 ounces) roasted red peppers, well drained

3 cups mixed baby lettuces *or* mixed greens (3 ounces)

½ cup crumbled mild feta *or* goat cheese

Pepper (optional)

Total preparation time: 20 minutes

1 Cut bread loaf horizontally in half; remove soft center from bottom half of bread, leaving 1-inch-thick shell.

2 In small bowl, combine mayonnaise, pesto and lemon juice; spread mixture on inside of bread shell.

3 Layer roast beef, red peppers, salad greens and cheese in bread shell. Season with pepper, if desired. Close with top of bread. Cut into 8 wedges.

Makes 8 servings.

1997 National Beef Cook-Off ®
★ *Winning Recipe* ★

Cook's Note

Basil pesto is an uncooked sauce made traditionally of fresh basil, garlic, pine nuts, Parmesan cheese and olive oil. It is available prepared in the supermarket.

Cook's Tip

If a round loaf diameter of bread is not readily available, special order it from your bakery.

Beef & Broccoli Slaw Wraps

- 1 pound 80% lean ground beef
- ¼ cup finely chopped onion
- ½ teaspoon salt
- ¼ teaspoon pepper
- 3 cups packaged broccoli *or* cabbage slaw mix
- ¼ cup hoisin sauce
- 4 medium flour tortillas, warmed

  Hoisin sauce (optional)

🕐 *Total preparation & cooking time: 20 minutes*

1 In large nonstick skillet, brown ground beef and onion over medium heat 8 to 10 minutes or until beef is no longer pink, breaking beef up into ½-inch crumbles. Pour off drippings. Season with salt and pepper. Stir in slaw mix and ¼ cup hoisin sauce; heat through.

2 Spoon ¼ of beef mixture (approximately 1 cup) in a row across center of each tortilla to within 1½ inches of right and left edges. Fold right and left edges of tortilla over filling, fold bottom edge up over filling, then roll up, jelly-roll fashion. Cut crosswise in half, if desired. Serve with hoisin sauce, if desired.

Makes 4 servings (serving size: 1 wrap).

Cook's Notes

Hoisin sauce is a thick, reddish-brown sauce that is a sweet and spicy mixture of soybeans, garlic, chili peppers and spices, used most often in Chinese cooking. Look for it in the ethnic section of the supermarket.

A medium tortilla is 8 to 10 inches in diameter.

Beef Soup Provençal

1 pound 80% lean ground beef

1 can (15 ounces) white beans, rinsed, drained

1 can ($13\frac{3}{4}$ to $14\frac{1}{2}$ ounces) ready-to-serve vegetable broth

1 can ($14\frac{1}{2}$ ounces) diced tomatoes with garlic, basil and oregano, undrained

$\frac{1}{2}$ teaspoon dried herbes de Provence, crushed

4 cups coarsely chopped fresh spinach *or* escarole

Shredded Parmesan cheese

Total preparation & cooking time: 20 minutes

1 In large saucepan, brown ground beef over medium heat 4 to 5 minutes or until outside surface is no longer pink, breaking up into $\frac{3}{4}$-inch crumbles. Pour off drippings.

2 Stir in beans, broth, tomatoes and herbes de Provence. Bring to a boil; reduce heat to low. Simmer, uncovered, 5 minutes. Stir in spinach. Continue simmering 5 minutes. Sprinkle with cheese.

Makes 4 servings (serving size: approx. $1\frac{1}{2}$ cups).

Cook's Note

Herbes de Provence are assorted dried herbs (usually including basil, fennel seed, lavender, marjoram, rosemary, sage, summer savory and thyme) that represent those most commonly used in the cooking of Southern France.

Cook's Tip

If herbes de Provence are not available, substitute a combination of $\frac{1}{4}$ teaspoon dried thyme leaves and $\frac{1}{4}$ teaspoon dried rosemary leaves, crushed.

Beef & Mushroom-Topped Potato Wedges

1 pound 80% lean ground beef

2 large all-purpose potatoes (approx. 10 ounces *each*)

2 cups sliced mushrooms

2 tablespoons chopped green onion

½ teaspoon salt

¼ teaspoon pepper

1 jar (12 ounces) beef gravy

½ cup dairy sour half-and-half

2 tablespoons sliced green onion (optional)

Total preparation & cooking time: 20 minutes

1 Pierce potatoes in several places with fork; place on paper towel in microwave oven. Microwave on HIGH 10 to 11 minutes or until tender; rearrange potatoes halfway through cooking.

2 Meanwhile in large nonstick skillet, brown ground beef, mushrooms and chopped green onion over medium heat 8 to 10 minutes or until beef is no longer pink, breaking beef up into ¾-inch crumbles. Pour off drippings. Season with salt and pepper. Reduce heat to low. Stir in gravy and sour half-and-half. Heat through; stir occasionally.

3 Cut potatoes lengthwise into quarters; cut each quarter crosswise in half. Arrange 4 potato pieces on each plate; top with ¼ of beef mixture. Sprinkle with sliced green onion, if desired.

Makes 4 servings.

Ginger Beef & Noodle Soup

1 pound 80% lean ground beef

½ teaspoon ground ginger

½ teaspoon salt

¼ to ½ teaspoon pepper

2 cups water

1 can (13¾ to 14½ ounces) ready-to-serve vegetable broth

1 package (3 ounces) beef-flavored instant ramen noodles, broken up

3 cups frozen broccoli stir-fry vegetable mixture

Total preparation & cooking time: 20 minutes

1 In Dutch oven, brown ground beef over medium heat 6 minutes or until outside surface is no longer pink, breaking up into ¾-inch crumbles. Pour off drippings. Season with ginger, salt and pepper.

2 Stir in water, broth and seasoning packet from ramen noodles; bring to a boil. Stir in noodles and vegetables; return to a boil. Continue cooking 2 to 3 minutes or until noodles are tender.

Makes 4 servings (serving size: approx. 1½ cups).

Cook's Note

Ramen noodles are packaged instant Asian dried noodles with seasonings included. When combined with boiling liquid, the noodles quickly rehydrate. These noodles are found in the ethnic or soup section of the supermarket.

Stir-Fried Steak & Vegetable Sandwiches

1 pound beef round tip steaks, cut ⅛ to ¼ inch thick

2 teaspoons olive oil

1 medium zucchini, cut into ¼-inch-thick slices

1 medium onion, thinly sliced

1 medium red bell pepper, cut into thin strips

1 teaspoon Italian seasoning, crushed

1 teaspoon olive oil

½ teaspoon salt

¼ teaspoon pepper

4 crusty hoagie rolls (approx. 6 inches long *each*), split

4 slices (1 ounce *each*) provolone cheese

🕐 *Total preparation & cooking time: 20 minutes*

1 Stack beef steaks; cut lengthwise in half, then crosswise into 1-inch-wide strips. Set aside.

2 In large nonstick skillet, heat 2 teaspoons oil over medium-high heat until hot. Add zucchini, onion, bell pepper and Italian seasoning. Stir-fry 3 to 4 minutes or until crisp-tender. Remove from skillet.

3 In same skillet, heat 1 teaspoon oil until hot. Stir-fry beef in 2 batches, 1 to 2 minutes each, or until outside surface is no longer pink. (Do not overcook.) Return beef to skillet. Season with salt and pepper. Stir in zucchini mixture; heat through.

4 Arrange ¼ of beef mixture on bottom of each roll; top each with 1 cheese slice. Place on rack in broiler pan so surface of cheese is 4 inches from heat. Broil 1 to 2 minutes or until cheese is melted. Close sandwiches.

Makes 4 servings (serving size: 1 sandwich).

15-Minute Pot Roast With Savory Potatoes

1 package fully cooked, ready-to-heat-and-eat boneless beef pot roast (1¾ to 2½ pounds)

Savory Potatoes

1 cup milk

2⅔ cups frozen mashed potatoes

½ cup prepared French onion, vegetable *or* green onion sour cream dip

🕐 *Total preparation & cooking time: 15 minutes*

1 Prepare pot roast according to package directions.

2 Meanwhile in medium saucepan, heat milk over medium heat 3 minutes or until steaming. (Do not boil.) Add potatoes. Cook and stir 5 minutes. Remove from heat. Add dip; stir to combine. Let stand, uncovered, 2 minutes.

3 Carve pot roast into slices. Serve with potatoes.

Makes 4 servings.

Cook's Note

Look for fully cooked, ready-to-heat-and-eat boneless beef pot roasts with natural juices in the meat department of your supermarket. They range from 1¾ to 2½ pounds and need only a quick heating in the microwave oven before serving.

Cook's Tip

Savory Potatoes recipe may be doubled.

Stir-Fried Beef Gyros In Pita Pockets

1 pound beef round tip steaks, cut ⅛ to ¼ inch thick

2 teaspoons olive oil

1 medium onion, halved, thinly sliced

1 teaspoon olive oil

2 cloves garlic, crushed

1 teaspoon dried oregano, crushed

¼ teaspoon salt

⅛ teaspoon pepper

4 pita pocket breads, halved crosswise, warmed

2 small tomatoes, thinly sliced

½ cup prepared cucumber ranch dressing

Total preparation & cooking time: 20 minutes

1 Stack beef steaks; cut lengthwise in half, then crosswise into 1-inch-wide strips. Set aside.

2 In large nonstick skillet, heat 2 teaspoons oil over medium-high heat until hot. Add onion. Stir-fry 3 to 4 minutes. Remove from skillet.

3 In same skillet, heat 1 teaspoon oil until hot. Stir-fry beef, garlic and oregano in 2 batches, 1 to 2 minutes each, or until outside surface of beef is no longer pink. (Do not overcook.) Return beef mixture to skillet. Season with salt and pepper. Stir in onion; heat through.

4 Fill pita pockets with equal amounts of tomatoes and beef mixture. Drizzle with dressing.

Makes 4 servings (serving size: 2 pita pocket halves).

Cook's Note

Round tip steaks, also called "minute," "breakfast," or "sandwich" steaks, cook very quickly; take care not to overcook or they will be dry.

Gorgonzola-Topped Tenderloin Steaks

4 beef tenderloin steaks, cut 1 inch thick (4 to 6 ounces *each*)

1 large clove garlic, crushed

¼ teaspoon cracked black pepper

½ cup ready-to-serve beef broth

¼ cup dry red wine

¼ cup crumbled Gorgonzola cheese

Total preparation & cooking time: 20 minutes

1 Heat large nonstick skillet 5 minutes over medium heat until hot. Combine garlic and pepper. Press evenly into both sides of each beef steak. Place steaks in skillet. Cook 10 to 13 minutes for medium rare to medium doneness; turn occasionally. Remove from skillet; keep warm.

2 In same skillet, add broth and wine; increase heat to medium-high. Cook and stir 1 to 2 minutes or until sauce is reduced by half.

3 Spoon sauce over steaks; sprinkle with cheese.

Makes 4 servings.

Cook's Note

Beef tenderloin steak is also called filet or filet mignon. These extremely tender, boneless steaks are cut from the whole tenderloin.

Cook's Tip

Other cheeses such as blue (or bleu) cheese, Roquefort or Stilton may be substituted for Gorgonzola.

Hurry-Up Beef & Mixed Vegetable Supper

- **1 pound beef cubed steaks**
- **1 teaspoon vegetable oil**
- **1 clove garlic, crushed**
- **¼ teaspoon salt**
- **¼ teaspoon pepper**
- **1 package (10 ounces) *or* 2 cups frozen mixed vegetables**
- **1 jar (12 ounces) mushroom gravy**
- **4 cornbread squares *or* split corn muffins**

Total preparation & cooking time: 15 minutes

1 Cut beef steaks lengthwise into 1-inch-wide strips, then crosswise into 1-inch pieces.

2 In large nonstick skillet, heat oil over medium heat until hot. Add beef and garlic. Cook and stir 5 to 6 minutes or until beef is no longer pink. (Do not overcook.) Season with salt and pepper.

3 Meanwhile place vegetables in 2-quart microwave-safe dish. Cover and microwave on HIGH 4 minutes; drain.

4 Add vegetables and gravy to beef. Cook over medium heat 1 to 2 minutes or until just heated through. Serve over cornbread.

Makes 4 servings.

Cook's Note

Cubed steaks, usually made from less tender cuts such as those from the bottom round or chuck, have been mechanically tenderized. They cook in minutes, instead of requiring long, slow cooking for tenderization.

Beef Pinwheels With Cucumber & Olives

¾ **pound thinly sliced deli roast beef**

1 **container (8 ounces) soft cream cheese with chives and onion**

4 **medium flour tortillas**

1 **cup finely chopped seeded cucumber**

2 **cans (4¼ ounces *each*) chopped pitted ripe olives**

🕐 *Total preparation time: 20 minutes*

1 Spread cream cheese evenly on one side of each tortilla. Top each with equal amounts of cucumber and olives. Layer deli roast beef over olives, leaving ½-inch border around edges. Roll up tightly.

2 To serve, cut each roll crosswise in half.

Makes 4 servings (serving size: 2 halves).

Cook's Tip

To serve as an appetizer, trim ends from each roll. Cut each roll crosswise into 8 slices.

Ranchero Beef & Rice Skillet

1 pound 80% lean ground beef

1 medium red *or* green bell pepper, cut into ½-inch pieces

1 large clove garlic, crushed

1 tablespoon chili powder

½ teaspoon salt

3 cups cooked rice, cooled

1 cup frozen peas, defrosted

¾ cup prepared salsa

Total preparation & cooking time: 20 minutes

1 In large nonstick skillet, brown ground beef, bell pepper and garlic over medium heat 8 to 10 minutes or until beef is no longer pink, breaking beef up into ¾-inch crumbles. Pour off drippings. Season with chili powder and salt.

2 Add rice to skillet; mix well. Continue cooking 2 minutes or until rice is hot; stir occasionally. Stir in peas and salsa; heat through.

Makes 4 servings.

Steak, Pear & Walnut Salad

3 cups cooked tender beef steak strips

1 package (10 ounces) mixed salad greens

1 firm ripe pear, cut into 12 wedges

¼ cup crumbled blue cheese

¼ cup coarsely chopped toasted walnuts

¼ cup prepared balsamic vinaigrette

 Total preparation time: 15 minutes

1 In large bowl, combine steak, greens, pear, cheese and walnuts. Drizzle with dressing; toss gently to coat. Serve immediately.

Makes 4 servings.

Cook's Note

Choose Anjou, Bartlett, Bosc or Comice pears, all widely available in supermarkets depending upon seasonality. Choose pears that are firm and fragrant without soft or blemished spots.

Cook's Tip

To toast walnuts, heat oven to 350°F. Spread walnuts in single layer in shallow baking pan. Bake 8 to 10 minutes or until golden; stir twice.

Easy Family Meals

Perhaps the family dinner—especially on a busy week-night—is the most difficult one for cooks to plan: it needs to be fast and have all-family appeal. These recipes are family favorites like pizza, pasta and pot roast, either made with just a few convenient ingredients teamed with quick-cooking beef cuts or ground beef, or with longer-cooking beef cuts in the slow cooker.

Sloppy Joe Biscuit Cups,
Page 59

Beef Stir-Fry With Green Beans & Noodles

1-pound high-quality beef top round steak, cut ¾ inch thick

½ cup water

¾ pound fresh green beans, cut into 2-inch pieces

3 cups water

2 packages (3 ounces *each*) instant ramen noodles, broken up

1 tablespoon vegetable oil

1 can (8 ounces) sliced water chestnuts, drained

½ cup ready-to-serve beef broth

Marinade

¼ cup soy sauce

1 tablespoon cornstarch

1 tablespoon dark sesame oil

2 teaspoons minced fresh ginger

Total preparation & cooking time: 30 minutes

1 Cut steak lengthwise in half, then crosswise into ⅛-inch-thick strips. In medium bowl, combine marinade ingredients. Add beef; stir to coat.

2 In wok or large skillet, bring ½ cup water to a boil over medium-high heat. Add green beans. Cover and cook 8 to 10 minutes or until tender. Remove beans with slotted spoon. In same pan, add 3 cups water; bring to a boil. Add noodles without seasoning packets. Cook 3 minutes. Drain and rinse noodles.

3 Remove beef from marinade; reserve marinade. Heat oil in same pan over medium-high heat until hot. Stir-fry beef in 2 batches, 1 to 2 minutes each, or until outside surface is no longer pink. (Do not overcook.)

4 Add beef, green beans, water chestnuts, broth and reserved marinade to pan. Bring to a boil; cook and stir 1 minute or until thickened. Add noodles to beef mixture; heat through.

Makes 4 servings.

Cook's Tip

Two cups frozen cut green beans may be substituted for fresh green beans.

43

Ranch Burgers

1½ pounds 80% lean
  ground beef

4 teaspoons Spicy
  Seasoning Mix *(recipe
  below)*

4 egg-bread hamburger
  buns, split

  Romaine lettuce

  Tomato slices

¼ cup prepared creamy
  ranch dressing

2 tablespoons canned
  French fried onions

Spicy Seasoning Mix

*Combine 2 teaspoons sweet
paprika, 2 teaspoons dried thyme
leaves, crushed, 1½ teaspoons
salt, 1 teaspoon garlic powder,
1 teaspoon onion powder,
½ teaspoon ground black pepper,
½ teaspoon ground red pepper
and ½ teaspoon ground white
pepper. Store in airtight container.
Shake before using to blend.*

Makes 3 tablespoons.

Total preparation & cooking time: 30 minutes

1 Prepare Spicy Seasoning Mix.

2 Shape ground beef into four ¾-inch-thick patties. Press Spicy Seasoning Mix evenly into both sides of each patty.

3 Heat large heavy nonstick skillet 5 minutes over medium heat until hot. Add patties to skillet. Cook 12 to 15 minutes to medium doneness (160°F) or until centers are no longer pink and juices show no pink color; turn once.

4 Line bottom of each bun with lettuce and tomato; top with burger. Spoon ranch dressing evenly over burgers; sprinkle with onions. Close sandwiches.

Makes 4 servings (serving size: 1 sandwich).

Mediterranean Beef Pot Roast & Vegetables

3 to 3 ¼ - pound boneless beef bottom round rump *or* chuck shoulder pot roast

8 new red potatoes (2 to 2 ½-inch diameter)

½ pound packaged baby carrots

4 whole cloves garlic

¼ cup water

¼ cup dry red wine

2 tablespoons cornstarch dissolved in 3 tablespoons water

Chopped fresh parsley

Seasoning

1 teaspoon dried rosemary leaves, crushed

1 teaspoon salt

½ teaspoon pepper

Total preparation & cooking time: 11½ hours

1 In slow cooker, place potatoes, carrots and garlic. In small bowl, combine seasoning ingredients. Press evenly into surface of beef pot roast. Place on top of vegetables. Add water and wine. Cover and cook on LOW 10 to 11 hours or until pot roast and vegetables are tender.

2 Remove pot roast and vegetables; keep warm. To make gravy, strain cooking liquid; skim fat. In small saucepan, combine 2 cups cooking liquid and cornstarch mixture. Bring to a boil; cook and stir 1 minute or until thickened.

3 Just before serving, carve pot roast across the grain into thin slices. Serve with vegetables and gravy. Garnish with parsley, as desired.

Makes 6 to 8 servings.

Cook's Note

Slow cooker recipes in this book were tested in 3½-, 4- and 5-quart slow cookers, which have a heat source around the side of the slow cooker. If you have a different type of slow cooker, refer to the manufacturer's directions for cooking times and temperatures.

Orange-Glazed Short Ribs With Rice & Peas

2½ pounds boneless beef chuck short ribs, cut into 4 x 2 x 2-inch pieces

1 large orange

1 cup prepared thick teriyaki baste and glaze sauce

½ cup water

2 cloves garlic, crushed

½ teaspoon pepper

2 teaspoons cornstarch dissolved in 1 tablespoon water

1 teaspoon dark sesame oil

Toasted slivered almonds *or* sesame seeds (optional)

Rice

1 cup uncooked regular long grain rice

1 cup frozen peas

Total preparation & cooking time: 9 hours

1 With vegetable peeler, remove three 3 x 1-inch strips of peel from orange. Squeeze ½ cup juice from orange; cover and refrigerate. In small bowl, combine orange peel, teriyaki sauce, water, garlic and pepper. In slow cooker, place beef short ribs. Pour teriyaki mixture over short ribs. Cover and cook on LOW 7½ to 8½ hours or until ribs are tender. (No stirring is necessary during cooking.)

2 Fifteen minutes before the end of cooking time, prepare rice according to package directions. Stir in peas; cover and keep warm.

3 Remove ribs from cooking liquid; keep warm. To make glaze, strain cooking liquid; skim fat. In small saucepan, combine 1 cup cooking liquid, reserved orange juice, cornstarch mixture and sesame oil. Bring to a boil; cook and stir 1 minute or until thickened.

4 Serve ribs with rice mixture and glaze. Sprinkle with almonds, if desired.

Makes 4 servings.

Cook's Tip

3 ¾ pounds bone-in beef chuck short ribs may be substituted for boneless short ribs.

Easy Steak Milanese

4 **beef cubed steaks (approx. 4 ounces** *each*)

½ **teaspoon salt**

¼ **teaspoon pepper**

1 **to 2 tablespoons olive oil**

¼ **cup chopped tomato**

Chopped fresh parsley (optional)

Coating

1 **egg**

1 **tablespoon water**

½ **cup seasoned dry bread crumbs**

2 **tablespoons grated Parmesan cheese**

🕐 *Total preparation & cooking time: 30 minutes*

1 Season beef steaks with salt and pepper. For coating, in shallow dish, beat egg and water until blended. In second shallow dish, combine bread crumbs and cheese. Dip each steak into egg mixture, allowing excess mixture to drain slightly, then dip into crumb mixture, coating both sides.

2 In large nonstick skillet, heat 1 tablespoon oil over medium-high heat until hot. Cook steaks in 2 batches, 5 to 6 minutes each, or until centers are no longer pink; turn once. Add remaining oil, if needed. Sprinkle with tomato and parsley, if desired.

Makes 4 servings.

Cook's Note

To chop means to cut foods into small irregular-sized pieces. Coarsely chopped refers to slightly larger pieces.

Southwest Beef & Chile Pizza

1997 National Beef Cook-Off ®
★ *Winning Recipe* ★

1 pound 80% lean ground beef

¼ teaspoon salt

1 package (16 ounces) prebaked thick pizza crust (12-inch diameter)

1 ¼ cups prepared thick and chunky salsa

1 ½ cups (6 ounces) shredded Mexican cheese blend *or* Monterey Jack cheese

1 can (4 ounces) diced green chilies, well drained

2 medium plum tomatoes, seeded, coarsely chopped

⅓ cup thin red onion slivers

2 tablespoons chopped fresh cilantro

Total preparation & cooking time: 35 minutes

1 Heat oven to 450°F. In large nonstick skillet, brown ground beef over medium heat 6 minutes or until outside surface is no longer pink, breaking up into ¾-inch crumbles. Pour off drippings. Season with salt.

2 Place pizza crust on ungreased large baking sheet. Spread salsa over crust; sprinkle with half of cheese. Top with beef, chilies, tomatoes, onion and remaining cheese.

3 Bake in 450°F oven 11 to 13 minutes or until toppings are hot and cheese is melted. Sprinkle with cilantro; cut into 8 wedges. Serve immediately.

Makes 1 pizza, 8 wedges.

Moroccan Beef Kabobs

1¼ pounds boneless beef
top sirloin steak, cut
1 inch thick

1 medium red bell pepper,
cut into 1-inch pieces

1 medium onion, cut into
1-inch pieces

½ teaspoon salt

2 cups hot cooked
couscous

Chopped fresh cilantro
(optional)

Seasoning

2 tablespoons chopped
fresh cilantro

2 tablespoons olive oil

3 large cloves garlic,
crushed

2 teaspoons ground cumin

1 teaspoon paprika

¼ teaspoon ground red
pepper

Total preparation & cooking time: 30 minutes

1 In medium bowl, combine seasoning ingredients. Cut beef steak into 1¼-inch pieces. Add beef, bell pepper and onion to seasoning mixture; toss to coat.

2 Alternately thread beef and vegetable pieces onto four 12-inch metal skewers.

3 Place skewers on rack in broiler pan so surface of beef is 3 to 4 inches from heat. Broil 8 to 10 minutes for medium rare to medium doneness; turn once. Season with salt. Serve kabobs with couscous. Garnish with cilantro, if desired.

Makes 4 servings (serving size: 1 kabob).

Fresh Tomato, Beef & Bow Tie Pasta

- **1 pound 80% lean ground beef**
- **3 cloves garlic, crushed**
- **2 cups chopped fresh tomatoes**
- **¾ teaspoon salt**
- **¼ teaspoon pepper**
- **1½ cups uncooked bow tie pasta**
- **2 tablespoons sliced fresh basil**
- **3 tablespoons grated Parmesan cheese**

 Total preparation & cooking time: 25 minutes

1 In large nonstick skillet, brown ground beef and garlic over medium heat 8 to 10 minutes or until beef is no longer pink, breaking beef up into ¾-inch crumbles. Pour off drippings.

2 Stir in tomatoes, salt and pepper. Cook over medium heat 5 minutes; stir occasionally.

3 Meanwhile cook pasta according to package directions. Toss beef mixture and basil with pasta. Sprinkle with cheese.

Makes 4 servings.

Cook's Note

Bow tie pasta is pasta that is shaped like small bow ties (also called farfalle).

Cook's Tip

One can (28 ounces) whole peeled plum tomatoes, drained and chopped, may be substituted for the fresh tomatoes.

Grecian Steak Salad

2 boneless beef top loin steaks, cut 1 inch thick (approx. 8 ounces *each*)

½ cup prepared Italian dressing

3 tablespoons finely crumbled feta *or* grated Parmesan cheese

3 tablespoons finely chopped kalamata *or* ripe olives

½ teaspoon salt

1 package (10 ounces) mixed salad greens (approx. 8 cups)

1 small cucumber, cut lengthwise in half, then crosswise into thin slices

¼ medium red onion, cut into thin wedges

Seasoning

1 teaspoon garlic powder

1 teaspoon dried oregano leaves, crushed

¼ teaspoon pepper

Total preparation & cooking time: 30 minutes

1 In small bowl, combine seasoning ingredients. Remove 1½ teaspoons seasoning mixture; press evenly into both sides of each beef steak. To remaining seasoning mixture, add dressing, cheese and olives; stir to mix.

2 Heat large nonstick skillet 5 minutes over medium heat until hot. Add steaks. Cook 12 to 15 minutes for medium rare to medium doneness; turn once. Carve steaks crosswise into thin slices. Season with salt.

3 In large bowl, combine salad greens, steak, cucumber, onion and dressing mixture; toss gently to coat. Serve immediately.

Makes 4 servings.

Easy "Meatballs," Vegetables & Pasta

Cook's Note

Penne pasta is made from large straight tubes of macaroni cut on the diagonal.

1 pound 80% lean ground beef

½ cup soft bread crumbs

1 egg, slightly beaten

2 tablespoons finely chopped onion

¼ teaspoon salt

⅛ teaspoon pepper

8 ounces uncooked penne pasta

3 cups (12 ounces) frozen Italian vegetable mixture

1 jar (approx. 26 ounces) prepared spaghetti sauce

2 tablespoons shredded Parmesan cheese

Total preparation & cooking time: 40 minutes

1 Heat oven to 375°F. In large bowl, combine ground beef, bread crumbs, egg, onion, salt and pepper; mix lightly but thoroughly. In 8-inch square baking dish, press beef mixture into ½-inch-thickness. Bake in 375°F oven 20 minutes to medium (160°F) or until center is no longer pink and juices show no pink color. Carefully pour off drippings. Cut beef mixture into 16 squares.

2 Meanwhile cook pasta according to package directions. Approximately 6 minutes before pasta is done, stir in vegetables. Drain; keep warm.

3 In large saucepan, combine "meatballs" and spaghetti sauce. Cook, uncovered, over medium-low heat 6 to 8 minutes or until heated through; stir occasionally. Serve over pasta and vegetables. Sprinkle with cheese.

Makes 4 servings.

Beef & Mushroom Risotto

1 pound 80% lean ground beef

1 package (5.5 to 5.6 ounces) risotto mix with garden vegetables

1½ cups sliced mushrooms

1 cup chopped red bell pepper

2 cloves garlic, crushed

½ teaspoon salt

¼ teaspoon pepper

2 tablespoons grated Parmesan cheese

1 tablespoon chopped fresh basil

Total preparation & cooking time: 30 minutes

1 Prepare risotto mix according to package directions.

2 Meanwhile in large nonstick skillet, brown ground beef, mushrooms, bell pepper and garlic over medium heat 8 to 10 minutes or until beef is no longer pink, breaking beef up into ¾-inch crumbles. Pour off drippings. Season with salt and pepper.

3 Stir risotto into beef mixture. Sprinkle with cheese and basil.

Makes 4 servings.

Cook's Tip

Look for packaged risotto mix in the rice section of the supermarket. Risotto may be flavored with ingredients such as vegetables, cheese, herbs, etc.

Tasty Taiwan-Ease Beef Salad

1997 National Beef Cook-Off ®
★ *Winning Recipe* ★

1¼ - pound boneless beef top sirloin steak, cut 1 inch thick

1 package (10 ounces) European *or* Italian-style mixed greens (approx. 8 cups)

1½ cups packaged shredded carrots

½ cup chopped unsalted dry roasted peanuts

Dressing

½ cup prepared Italian dressing

2 tablespoons soy sauce

1 teaspoon grated fresh ginger

¼ teaspoon crushed red pepper

Total preparation & cooking time: 30 minutes

1 In small bowl, combine dressing ingredients. Cut beef steak lengthwise in half, then crosswise into ¼-inch-thick strips. In medium bowl, combine beef and 2 tablespoons dressing mixture; toss to coat. Let stand 10 minutes.

2 Meanwhile in large bowl, combine mixed greens, carrots and peanuts; toss gently. Set aside.

3 In large nonstick skillet, heat 2 tablespoons dressing mixture over medium-high heat until hot. Stir-fry beef in 2 batches, 2 to 3 minutes each, or until outside surface is no longer pink. Arrange beef on salad. Drizzle with remaining dressing mixture.

Makes 4 servings.

Sloppy Joe Biscuit Cups

1 pound 80% lean ground beef

¼ cup finely chopped celery

¼ cup finely chopped onion

¼ cup finely chopped green bell pepper

½ cup prepared barbecue sauce

¼ teaspoon salt

1 can (12 ounces) refrigerated flaky buttermilk biscuits

5 slices (1 ounce *each*) Cheddar cheese, quartered

Total preparation & cooking time: 35 minutes

1 Heat oven to 400°F. In large nonstick skillet, brown ground beef, celery, onion and bell pepper over medium heat 6 minutes or until outside surface of beef is no longer pink, breaking beef up into ½-inch crumbles. Pour off drippings. Stir in barbecue sauce and salt. Simmer, uncovered, 2 to 3 minutes; stir occasionally.

2 Meanwhile place 1 biscuit into each of 10 ungreased standard-sized muffin cups; press dough firmly onto bottoms and up sides of cups. Spoon approximately ¼ cup beef mixture into each biscuit cup.

3 Bake in 400°F oven 10 to 12 minutes or until edges of biscuits are golden brown. Arrange 2 pieces of cheese on top of each biscuit cup. Continue baking 1 to 2 minutes or until cheese is melted. Let stand 1 minute. Loosen edges of biscuit cups before removing from pan.

Makes 10 biscuit cups.

Cook's Tips

Five slices (¾ ounce each) American cheese may be substituted for Cheddar cheese.

To reheat one biscuit cup, place on microwave-safe dish. Microwave on HIGH 30 to 45 seconds.

Thai-Style Steak Pizza

1¼-pound boneless beef
   top sirloin steak, cut
   1 inch thick

1 tablespoon roasted
   garlic oil

¼ cup sliced green onions

1 package (10 ounces)
   prebaked thin pizza crust
   (12-inch diameter)

3 tablespoons prepared
   Thai peanut sauce

1½ cups (6 ounces) shredded
   pizza cheese blend

½ cup packaged shredded
   carrots

2 tablespoons chopped
   fresh cilantro

Total preparation & cooking time: 30 minutes

1 Heat oven to 425°F. Cut beef steak lengthwise in half, then crosswise into ¼-inch-thick strips. In large nonstick skillet, heat oil over medium-high heat until hot. Stir-fry beef and onions in 2 batches, 2 to 3 minutes each, or until outside surface of beef is no longer pink. Remove from skillet with slotted spoon.

2 Place pizza crust on ungreased large baking sheet. Spread with peanut sauce; sprinkle with ½ cup of cheese. Top with beef mixture; sprinkle with remaining 1 cup of cheese. Bake in 425°F oven 11 to 13 minutes or until cheese is melted. Sprinkle with carrots and cilantro. Cut into 8 wedges. Serve immediately.

Makes 1 pizza, 8 wedges.

Cook's Notes

Cilantro is an herb with bright green leaves and earthy flavor widely used in Asian, Caribbean and Latin American cooking. It is available year round in most supermarkets. Also called coriander and Chinese parsley.

Thai peanut sauce is a Southeast Asian sauce usually made of peanut butter, oil, garlic, onion, chilies and soy sauce. Look for it in the ethnic section of the supermarket.

Sunday Suppers

Chapter 3

Remember when Sunday supper meant the whole family gathering 'round and enjoying a meal together? Didn't have to be fancy — it was the camaraderie that counted. Sunday suppers are back and these recipes feature some of the old favorites like meatloaf, chili, pot pie and stew — but all have been deliciously updated for the contemporary Sunday night crowd.

Puff Pastry-Topped Beef Pot Pie, Page 79

Three-Mushroom Meatloaf

1½ pounds 80% lean ground beef

2 teaspoons butter

½ cup finely chopped onion

8 ounces assorted wild *or* button mushrooms, sliced

3 cloves garlic, crushed

¾ cup soft bread crumbs

1 egg, slightly beaten

1 teaspoon salt

¾ teaspoon dried thyme leaves, crushed

¼ teaspoon pepper

Pepper Gravy

1 teaspoon butter

½ cup diced red, yellow *or* green bell pepper

1 jar (12 ounces) beef gravy

½ teaspoon dried thyme leaves, crushed

Total preparation & cooking time: 1½ hours

1 Heat oven to 350°F. In large nonstick skillet, heat 2 teaspoons butter over medium heat until hot. Add onion. Cook and stir 3 minutes. Add mushrooms and garlic. Cook and stir 6 to 8 minutes or until mushrooms are tender. Remove from heat; cool 5 minutes.

2 In large bowl, combine ground beef, bread crumbs, egg, salt, ¾ teaspoon thyme, pepper and mushroom mixture; mix lightly but thoroughly.

3 On rack in broiler pan, shape beef mixture into 8 x 4-inch loaf. Bake in 350°F oven approximately 1¼ hours to medium doneness (160°F) or until center is no longer pink and juices show no pink color.

4 Meanwhile prepare Pepper Gravy. In medium saucepan, heat 1 teaspoon butter over medium heat until hot. Add bell pepper. Cook and stir 5 minutes or until crisp-tender. Add gravy and thyme; heat through. Carve meatloaf into slices. Serve with gravy.

Makes 6 servings.

Cook's Note

Due to the natural nitrate content of certain ingredients often used in meatloaf, such as onions, celery and bell peppers, meatloaf may remain pink even if a 160°F internal temperature has been reached. Always check the internal temperature using a meat thermometer or instant-read thermometer to be certain it reaches 160°F.

Cook's Tip

A combination of mushrooms such as shiitake, cremini (brown) and button may be used.

Shredded Beef & Chorizo Sausage Hash

2 cups shredded cooked beef, chopped (beef chuck preferred)

8 ounces fresh chorizo sausage, casing removed

1 tablespoon vegetable oil

¾ cup finely chopped green bell pepper

¾ cup finely chopped onion

3 cups frozen potatoes O'Brien, defrosted

¼ teaspoon salt

⅓ cup ready-to-serve beef broth

3 tablespoons chopped fresh cilantro

Total preparation & cooking time: 50 minutes

1 Heat oven to 400°F. In large ovenproof non-stick skillet, brown sausage over medium heat 8 to 10 minutes, breaking up into ½-inch crumbles. Drain on paper towels.

2 Discard drippings; wipe out skillet. In same skillet, heat oil over medium heat until hot. Add bell pepper and onion. Cook and stir until tender. Stir in potatoes. Season with salt.

3 Add beef, sausage, broth and cilantro to vegetables; mix well. Firmly press down top of mixture. Bake in 400°F oven 20 minutes or until lightly browned and crisp.

Makes 6 servings.

Cook's Note

Chorizo sausage is a highly seasoned, coarsely ground pork sausage flavored with garlic, chili pepper and other spices.

Braised Beef With Mushrooms & Barley

3 - pound boneless beef chuck pot roast (arm, blade *or* shoulder)

1 tablespoon vegetable oil

1 teaspoon salt

¼ teaspoon pepper

½ pound medium cremini *or* button mushrooms, halved

1 medium onion, chopped

3 large cloves garlic, crushed

1¼ cups ready-to-serve beef broth

1 bay leaf

½ cup medium pearl barley

1 cup frozen peas, defrosted

⅓ cup dairy sour cream (optional)

Total preparation & cooking time: 3 hours

1 In Dutch oven, heat oil over medium heat until hot. Add beef pot roast; brown evenly. Remove pot roast. Season with salt and pepper.

2 In same pan, add mushrooms, onion and garlic. Cook and stir until onion is lightly browned. Add pot roast, broth and bay leaf. Bring to a boil; reduce heat to low. Cover tightly and simmer gently 1½ hours.

3 Add barley. Cover tightly and continue simmering 45 to 60 minutes or until pot roast and barley are tender. Remove pot roast; keep warm. Remove bay leaf.

4 Add peas and sour cream, if desired, to barley mixture. Cook and stir until just heated through. Carve pot roast into thin slices; serve with barley mixture.

Makes 8 servings.

Cook's Notes

Pearl barley is medium, long-cooking barley, the kind traditionally used in recipes that benefit from long simmering; quick barley cooks in 10 to 12 minutes. They are not interchangeable in recipes.

Cremini mushrooms are a darker brown, slightly firmer and richer-tasting version of the familiar white button mushrooms.

Meatball & Veggie Sandwiches

2 pounds 80% lean ground beef

8 French bread rolls (6 inches long *each*)

2 eggs, slightly beaten

¼ cup finely chopped onion

2 cloves garlic, crushed

1 teaspoon salt

¼ teaspoon pepper

1 medium green *or* red bell pepper

1 medium onion

1 tablespoon vegetable oil

2½ cups prepared spaghetti sauce with basil

½ cup (2 ounces) shredded mozzarella cheese

Total preparation & cooking time: 1 hour

1 Heat oven to 350°F. Cut French bread horizontally in half to within ½ inch of one side. Remove small amount of soft center from bottom and top of each piece. Use bread removed from center to make 1 cup crumbs.

2 Combine ground beef, bread crumbs, eggs, onion, garlic, salt and pepper; mix lightly but thoroughly. Shape beef mixture into 24 meatballs. Place meatballs on rack in broiler pan. Bake in 350°F oven 25 to 30 minutes or until centers are no longer pink and juices show no pink color.

3 Meanwhile cut bell pepper and medium onion into thin strips. Heat oil in large nonstick skillet over medium heat until hot. Cook vegetables 8 to 10 minutes or until crisp-tender; stir occasionally. Add meatballs and spaghetti sauce to vegetables. Cook, uncovered, over medium-low heat until heated through.

4 To serve, place 3 meatballs and equal amount of sauce mixture on bottom half of each roll. Sprinkle with equal amounts of cheese. Close sandwich.

Makes 8 servings (serving size: 1 sandwich).

Bold & Beefy Black Bean Chili

3 pounds boneless beef chuck, cut into ½-inch pieces

2 tablespoons vegetable oil

½ teaspoon salt

2 cans (14½ to 16 ounces *each*) Mexican-style stewed tomatoes, undrained

½ cup prepared steak sauce

½ cup water

3 tablespoons chili powder

¼ teaspoon crushed red pepper

2 cans (15 ounces *each*) black beans, rinsed, drained

Toppings (optional)

  Sliced green onions

  Dairy sour cream

  Shredded Cheddar cheese

Total preparation & cooking time: 2 hours

1 In Dutch oven, heat oil over medium-high heat until hot. Cook and stir beef in 4 batches; brown evenly. Pour off drippings. Return beef to pan. Season with salt.

2 Stir in tomatoes, steak sauce, water, chili powder and red pepper. Bring to a boil; reduce heat to low. Cover tightly and simmer gently 1¼ to 1½ hours or until beef is tender. Stir in beans; heat through.

3 Serve with toppings, if desired.

Makes 8 servings (serving size: approx. 1 cup).

Cook's Tip

The secret to tender beef is to simmer gently in a tightly covered pan without boiling, until the meat is fork-tender.

Beef & Couscous Stuffed Roasted Peppers

- 1 **pound 80% lean ground beef**
- 4 **large red *or* yellow bell peppers (7 to 9 ounces *each*), cut lengthwise in half, seeded**
- 1 **cup chopped zucchini**
- ¼ **teaspoon salt**
- ¼ **teaspoon pepper**
- 1¼ **cups water**
- 1 **package (5.8 ounces) olive oil and garlic-flavored couscous mix**
- 2 **tablespoons coarsely chopped pitted kalamata *or* ripe olives**
- ¼ **cup crumbled feta cheese**

Total preparation & cooking time: 40 minutes

1 Heat oven to 450°F. In 15 x 10-inch jelly-roll pan, arrange bell peppers, cut-side down. Bake in 450°F oven 10 to 15 minutes or until peppers begin to brown. Set aside.

2 Meanwhile in large nonstick skillet, brown ground beef and zucchini over medium heat 8 to 10 minutes or until beef is no longer pink, breaking beef up into ½-inch crumbles. Pour off drippings. Season with salt and pepper.

3 Stir water and seasoning packet from couscous mix into beef mixture. Bring to a boil. Stir in couscous; remove from heat. Cover and let stand 5 minutes. Stir in olives.

4 Spoon beef mixture evenly into each pepper half; sprinkle with cheese.

Makes 4 servings (serving size: 2 stuffed pepper halves).

Cook's Note

Couscous is a tiny granulated precooked and packaged pasta sold in supermarkets and Middle Eastern markets. It may be plain or flavored. Look for it with the pasta or grains or in the ethnic section of the supermarket.

Beef & Winter Vegetable Stew

2 pounds beef for stew, cut into 1-inch pieces

2 tablespoons vegetable oil

2 cups chopped onions

½ teaspoon salt

¼ teaspoon pepper

1 can (13¾ to 14½ ounces) ready-to-serve beef broth

1 cup dark beer *or* nonalcoholic beer

1 pound small red potatoes, quartered

3 medium carrots, cut into ½-inch pieces

2 tablespoons cornstarch dissolved in 3 tablespoons water

Chopped fresh parsley (optional)

Total preparation & cooking time: 2 hours

1 In Dutch oven, heat oil over medium heat until hot. Cook and stir beef and onions in 2 batches; brown evenly. Pour off drippings. Return beef and onions to pan. Season with salt and pepper.

2 Stir in broth and beer. Bring to a boil; reduce heat to low. Cover tightly and simmer gently 1¼ hours.

3 Add vegetables. Bring to a boil; reduce heat to low. Cover tightly and continue simmering 20 to 30 minutes or until beef and vegetables are tender.

4 Stir in cornstarch mixture. Bring to a boil; cook and stir 1 minute or until thickened. Garnish with parsley, if desired.

Makes 6 servings (serving size: approx. 1½ cups).

Cook's Notes

Browning beef prior to cooking adds rich color and flavor to the dish. Follow these tips.

- *Pat pieces of beef for stew dry with paper toweling for better browning. Brown beef slowly on all sides; a slow browning adheres better than a quick browning.*
- *Do not crowd the beef in the pan. Brown in batches; otherwise, the beef will steam instead of brown.*

Cooking in liquid, also called stewing, refers to simmering beef gently in enough liquid to cover the beef and other ingredients in a tightly covered pan. The steam created in the pan helps ensure moist, fork-tender beef. Boiling will not speed the cooking; it only results in tough, dry beef.

Braising is a similar cooking method used for larger cuts of beef such as pot roast. Only a small amount of liquid is added for braising because the large piece of beef and other ingredients create liquid as they simmer.

Savory Beef Empanadas & Pickled Red Onions

Pickled Red Onions

*In medium bowl, combine
1/4 cup packed brown sugar,
2 tablespoons cider vinegar and
1/2 teaspoon salt; stir until sugar
is partially dissolved. Cut 1 medium red onion crosswise in half,
then cut into thin slices. Add to
sugar mixture; toss to mix. Cover
and refrigerate 1 hour or
overnight; stir occasionally.*

Makes approx. 1 1/2 cups.

- 1 **pound 80% lean ground beef**

  Pickled Red Onions (*see recipe at left*)
- 1/3 **cup raisins**
- 1/4 **cup dry sherry *or* apple juice**
- 3 **cloves garlic, crushed**
- 1 1/2 **teaspoons ground cumin**
- 1/4 **teaspoon salt**
- 3/4 **cup (3 ounces) shredded jalapeño pepper cheese**
- 1 **package (15 ounces) refrigerated pie crusts**

  Water
- 1 **egg, beaten**

*Total preparation & cooking time: 45 minutes
Chilling time: 1 hour or overnight*

1 Prepare Pickled Red Onions.

2 In small bowl, combine raisins and sherry. Set aside.

3 In large nonstick skillet, brown ground beef and garlic over medium heat 6 minutes or until outside surface of beef is no longer pink, breaking beef up into 1/2-inch crumbles. Pour off drippings. Stir in cumin, salt and reserved raisin mixture. Continue cooking 1 minute; cool slightly. Stir in cheese.

4 Heat oven to 400°F. Cut each pie crust circle in half; place on ungreased baking sheet. Spoon 1/4 of beef mixture onto one side of each pastry piece, leaving 1/2-inch border at edges. Moisten edges with water; fold pastry over filling. Crimp with fork to seal.

5 Brush tops lightly with egg. Bake in 400°F oven 16 to 18 minutes or until golden. Serve with Pickled Red Onions.

Makes 4 servings (serving size: 1 empanada).

Hungarian Round Steak & Spaetzle

2¼ to 2½ - pound high-quality, full-cut beef round steak, cut ¾ inch thick

2 tablespoons flour

½ teaspoon salt

¼ teaspoon pepper

2 tablespoons vegetable oil

1 can (13¾ to 14½ ounces) ready-to-serve beef broth

5 teaspoons sweet Hungarian *or* regular paprika

2 medium onions, cut crosswise into ½-inch-thick slices, separated into rings

1 package (9 to 10½ ounces) uncooked spaetzle

2 teaspoons flour dissolved in 2 tablespoons cold water

⅔ cup dairy sour cream

Chopped fresh parsley (optional)

Total preparation & cooking time: 2 hours

1 Cut beef steak into 6 equal pieces. In shallow dish, combine 2 tablespoons flour, salt and pepper. Lightly coat both sides of beef pieces with flour mixture. Shake off excess flour mixture.

2 In large nonstick skillet, heat oil over medium heat until hot. Cook beef in 2 batches; brown evenly. Pour off drippings.

3 Add broth and paprika. Bring to a boil; reduce heat to low. Return beef to pan. Cover tightly and simmer gently 45 minutes. Add onions; spoon cooking liquid over onions and beef. Cover tightly and continue simmering 30 to 40 minutes or until beef is tender. Remove beef and onions; keep warm. Meanwhile prepare spaetzle according to package directions.

4 Skim fat from cooking liquid. In same pan, combine 1½ cups cooking liquid and flour mixture. Bring to a boil; cook and stir 1 minute or until thickened. Remove from heat; whisk in sour cream. Serve sauce with beef, onions and spaetzle. Garnish with parsley, if desired.

Makes 6 servings.

Cook's Note

Spaetzle are small dumplings or noodles found in the pasta section of the supermarket.

Cook's Tip

Four cups cooked medium egg noodles may be substituted for spaetzle.

Beef Enchiladas

1 pound 80% lean ground beef

½ cup chopped onion

2 cloves garlic, crushed

½ teaspoon salt

¼ teaspoon pepper

2 cans (10 ounces *each*) mild enchilada sauce

8 small corn tortillas

¾ cup (3 ounces) shredded jalapeño pepper cheese

1 tablespoon chopped fresh cilantro

Dairy sour cream (optional)

Total preparation & cooking time: 45 minutes

1 Heat oven to 350°F. In large nonstick skillet, brown ground beef, onion and garlic over medium heat 6 minutes or until outside surface of beef is no longer pink, breaking beef up into ½-inch crumbles. Pour off drippings. Season with salt and pepper. Stir in ½ cup enchilada sauce from one can. Set aside remaining sauce from that can.

2 Pour second can enchilada sauce into shallow dish. Dip tortillas, one at a time, into sauce to coat both sides. Spoon beef mixture evenly down centers of each tortilla; roll up. Place seam-side down in 12 x 8-inch baking dish.

3 Cover with aluminum foil. Bake in 350°F oven 15 minutes. Remove aluminum foil. Spoon reserved enchilada sauce over enchiladas; sprinkle with cheese. Continue baking, uncovered, 10 minutes or until cheese is melted. Sprinkle with cilantro. Serve with sour cream, if desired.

Makes 4 servings (serving size: 2 enchiladas).

Cook's Notes

Enchiladas are a Mexican dish in which a softened corn tortilla is wrapped around a filling of meat or cheese. It is usually served hot, topped with a tomato-based sauce.

A small tortilla is 6 to 7 inches in diameter.

Easy Beef Cassoulet

1¼ pounds boneless beef top sirloin steak, cut ¾ inch thick

1 tablespoon olive oil

½ teaspoon salt

¼ teaspoon pepper

1½ teaspoons olive oil

2 medium carrots, cut into ¼-inch-thick slices

2 small onions, *each* cut lengthwise into 8 wedges

8 ounces cremini *or* button mushrooms, quartered

¼ cup dry white wine

1 can (16 ounces) small white beans, rinsed, drained

1 can (14½ ounces) diced tomatoes with garlic and onion, undrained

Total preparation & cooking time: 35 minutes

1 Cut beef steak into ¾-inch pieces. In large non-stick skillet, heat 1 tablespoon oil over medium-high heat until hot. Stir-fry beef in 2 batches, 1 to 2 minutes each, or until outside surface is no longer pink. Remove from skillet. Season with salt and pepper.

2 In same skillet, heat 1½ teaspoons oil over medium heat until hot. Add carrots and onions. Stir-fry 5 minutes or until crisp-tender. Stir in mushrooms and wine. Continue stir-frying 5 minutes. Stir in beans and tomatoes. Continue cooking 3 minutes.

3 Return beef to skillet. Cook 2 minutes or until just heated through. (Do not overcook.)

Makes 4 servings (serving size: approx. 2 cups).

Puff Pastry-Topped Beef Pot Pie

1¼-pound boneless beef top sirloin steak, cut ¾ inch thick

½ package (17¼ ounces) frozen puff pastry (1 sheet), defrosted

1 egg yolk beaten with 1 tablespoon water (optional)

1 tablespoon vegetable oil

¼ teaspoon pepper

¼ teaspoon dried thyme leaves, crushed

1 tablespoon vegetable oil

1 package (16 ounces) frozen vegetables (broccoli, cauliflower and red pepper)

¼ cup chopped onion

1 jar (12 ounces) beef gravy

🕐 *Total preparation & cooking time: 30 minutes*

1 Heat oven to 400°F. Unfold puff pastry sheet on lightly floured surface. Cut out four 4-inch circles; place on ungreased baking sheet. Cut decorative pieces from pastry scraps; arrange on pastry circles. Brush pastry with egg yolk wash, if desired. Bake in 400°F oven 12 to 14 minutes or until golden brown. Transfer to wire rack.

2 Meanwhile cut beef steak lengthwise in thirds, then crosswise into ½-inch-thick strips. In large nonstick skillet, heat 1 tablespoon oil over medium-high heat until hot. Stir-fry beef in 2 batches, 1 to 2 minutes each, or until outside surface is no longer pink. Season with pepper and thyme.

3 In same skillet, heat remaining 1 tablespoon oil until hot. Add vegetables and onion. Stir-fry 5 to 6 minutes or until vegetables are tender. Reduce heat to medium. Stir in gravy and beef. Cook until just heated through. Divide beef mixture among 4 bowls or plates (approximately 1 cup each); top with puff pastry.

Makes 4 servings (serving size: 1 pot pie).

Cook's Tip

One package (16 ounces) frozen broccoli, cauliflower and carrots may be substituted for broccoli, cauliflower and red pepper. Stir-fry vegetables 8 to 10 minutes or until tender.

Corned Beef, Broccoli & Swiss Cheese Pockets

½ **pound fully cooked corned beef, cut into ½-inch cubes**

1 **tablespoon butter**

½ **cup chopped onion**

1½ **cups frozen cut broccoli, defrosted**

1 **cup (4 ounces) shredded Swiss cheese**

¼ **teaspoon pepper**

1 **package (10 ounces) refrigerated pizza dough**

2 **tablespoons prepared Thousand Island dressing**

🕐 *Total preparation & cooking time: 30 minutes*

1 Heat oven to 425°F. In medium nonstick skillet, heat butter until hot. Add onion. Cook and stir 2 to 3 minutes or until tender. Remove from heat. Add corned beef, broccoli, cheese and pepper; mix well.

2 On ungreased baking sheet, unroll pizza dough; cut into quarters. Press each quarter into 6 x 5-inch rectangles. Spread each with ½ tablespoon of dressing to within 1 inch of edges. Divide corned beef mixture evenly onto centers of each piece of dough. Bring together 2 opposite corners of dough; pinch to seal. Loosely close straight edges of dough to form a diamond shape. (Edges do not need to be completely sealed.)

3 Bake in 425°F oven 11 to 13 minutes or until golden brown.

Makes 4 servings (serving size: 1 pocket).

Easy Beef, Vegetable &
Tortellini Soup, Page 85

Cook Once,
Dine Twice

Chapter 4

Cooking once to dine twice

adds up to dividend meals.

Look at the options. A basic

beef mixture prepared in

the slow cooker is divided;

a few ingredients are added

and you have two entirely

different dishes. Or, cook

extra, and use the "planned"

leftovers to create something

brand new. These recipes

show you how!

Two-Way Shredded Beef

Tex-Mex Beef Wraps With Tomato-Corn Salsa

Honey-Mustard BBQ Beefwiches

3 to 3¼-pound boneless beef chuck shoulder pot roast *or* bottom round roast, cut into 4 large chunks

1 medium onion, quartered

3 cloves garlic

1 teaspoon salt

½ teaspoon pepper

¾ cup water

Cook's Tips

Beef mixture may be frozen up to 3 months in covered container; defrost in refrigerator before using.

Large flour tortillas used in Tex-Mex Beef Wraps With Tomato-Corn Salsa are 11 to 12 inches in diameter.

Total preparation & cooking time: 10 hours

1 In slow cooker, place onion and garlic; top with beef chunks. Sprinkle with salt and pepper; add water. Cover and cook on LOW 9 to 9½ hours or until beef is tender. (No stirring is necessary during cooking.)

2 Remove beef from cooking liquid; cool slightly. Meanwhile strain cooking liquid and skim fat. Set aside. Trim and discard excess fat from cooked beef. Shred beef with 2 forks.

3 Divide shredded beef in half (approximately 3¾ cups per portion); add ¼ cup reserved cooking liquid to each portion. Use one portion to prepare Tex-Mex Beef Wraps With Tomato-Corn Salsa or Honey-Mustard BBQ Beefwiches. Cover and refrigerate remaining portion up to 4 days for later use.

Makes approx. 7½ cups shredded beef.

Tex-Mex Beef Wraps With Tomato-Corn Salsa

1 portion (approx. 3¾ cups) Two-Way Shredded Beef

1 jar (16 ounces) prepared thick and chunky salsa

2 tablespoons chopped cilantro

4 large flour tortillas, warmed

Chopped fresh cilantro

Tomato-Corn Salsa

½ cup frozen whole corn kernels, defrosted

1 small tomato, chopped

1 tablespoon chopped cilantro

Total preparation & cooking time: 20 minutes

1 In small bowl, combine Tomato-Corn Salsa ingredients with 2 tablespoons thick and chunky salsa. Cover and refrigerate until ready to use.

2 In slow cooker removable crock or 1½-quart microwave-safe dish, combine one portion shredded beef, remaining thick and chunky salsa and 2 tablespoons chopped cilantro. Cover and microwave on HIGH 7 to 8 minutes (8 to 9 minutes, if refrigerated) or until hot; stir once.

3 Spoon ¼ of beef mixture evenly over each tortilla, leaving 1½-inch border on all sides. Top each with approximately ¼ cup Tomato-Corn Salsa. Fold right and left edges of tortilla over filling; fold bottom edge up over filling. Roll up jelly-roll fashion. Garnish with chopped cilantro. Serve immediately.

Makes 4 servings (serving size: 1 wrap).

Honey-Mustard BBQ Beefwiches

1 portion (approx. 3¾ cups) Two-Way Shredded Beef

1 cup prepared honey mustard barbecue sauce

4 hamburger buns *or* kaiser rolls, split

¼ cup chopped green bell pepper

¼ cup chopped sweet onion

Total preparation & cooking time: 15 minutes

1 In slow cooker removable crock or 1½-quart microwave-safe dish, combine one portion shredded beef and barbecue sauce; mix thoroughly. Cover and microwave on HIGH 5 to 6 minutes (6 to 7 minutes, if refrigerated) or until hot; stir once.

2 Place equal amounts of beef mixture on bottom half of each bun. Top with bell pepper and onion. Close sandwiches.

Makes 4 servings (serving size: 1 sandwich).

Double Batch Beef & Beans

10-Minute Beefy Chili

Easy Beef, Vegetable & Tortellini Soup

2½ **pounds beef for stew, cut into ¾-inch pieces**

2 **cans (14½ ounces *each*) diced tomatoes with garlic and onions, undrained**

1 **can (15½ ounces) great Northern beans, rinsed, drained**

1 **can (15½ ounces) kidney beans, rinsed, drained**

1 **teaspoon salt**

½ **teaspoon pepper**

Cook's Tip

Beef mixture may be frozen up to 3 months in covered container; defrost in refrigerator before using.

Total preparation & cooking time: 9¼ hours

1 In slow cooker, combine all ingredients; mix thoroughly. Cover and cook on LOW 8 to 9 hours or until beef is tender. (No stirring is necessary during cooking.)

2 Divide beef mixture in half (approximately 5 cups per portion). Use one portion of beef mixture to prepare 10-Minute Beefy Chili or Easy Beef, Vegetable & Tortellini Soup. Cover and refrigerate remaining portion up to 4 days for later use.

Makes approx. 10 cups beef mixture.

10-Minute Beefy Chili

**1 portion (approx. 5 cups)
Double Batch Beef & Beans**

**1 jar (16 ounces) prepared
picante sauce *or* thick and
chunky salsa**

2 teaspoons chili powder

Toppings (optional)

Dairy sour cream

Chopped green onion

⊖ *Total preparation & cooking time: 10 minutes*

1 In large saucepan, combine beef mixture, picante sauce and chili powder. Cook over medium-high heat 5 to 6 minutes (7 to 8 minutes, if refrigerated) or until hot; stir occasionally.

2 Top with sour cream and green onion, if desired.

Makes 4 servings (serving size: approx. 1²/₃ cups).

Cook's Tip

Recipe may be doubled; prepare in Dutch oven.

Easy Beef, Vegetable & Tortellini Soup

**1 portion (approx. 5 cups)
Double Batch Beef & Beans**

**2 cans (13³/₄ to 14¹/₂ ounces
each) ready-to-serve beef
broth**

**2 cups frozen vegetable
mixture**

1 cup frozen cheese tortellini

**³/₄ teaspoon dried Italian
seasoning, crushed**

Grated Parmesan cheese

⊖ *Total preparation & cooking time: 15 minutes*

1 In large saucepan or Dutch oven, combine beef mixture, broth, vegetables, tortellini and Italian seasoning. Bring to a boil; reduce heat to medium. Cook 8 to 10 minutes (10 to 12 minutes, if refrigerated) or until vegetables and tortellini are tender; stir occasionally.

2 Sprinkle with cheese, as desired.

Makes 4 servings (serving size: approx. 2¹/₄ cups).

Cook's Tip

Use a frozen vegetable mixture such as broccoli, red peppers, onions and mushrooms.

Favorite Family Meatloaf

Favorite Family Meatloaf

Southern BBQ Meatloaf Sandwiches

2 **pounds 80% lean ground beef**

1 **cup soft bread crumbs**

¾ **cup finely chopped onion**

½ **cup milk**

1 **large clove garlic, crushed**

1 **egg, slightly beaten**

1 **teaspoon salt**

½ **teaspoon pepper**

½ **teaspoon dried thyme leaves, crushed**

⅓ **cup prepared barbecue sauce**

Cook's Note

Due to the natural nitrate content of certain ingredients often used in meatloaf, such as onions, celery and bell peppers, meatloaf may remain pink even if a 160°F internal temperature has been reached. Always check the internal temperature using a meat thermometer or instant-read thermometer to be certain it reaches 160°F.

Total preparation & cooking time: 1½ hours

1 Heat oven to 350°F. In large bowl, combine all ingredients except barbecue sauce; mix lightly but thoroughly.

2 On rack in broiler pan, shape beef mixture into 10 x 4-inch loaf. Bake in 350°F oven 1 hour and 10 minutes. Generously brush meatloaf with barbecue sauce. Continue baking 5 to 10 minutes to medium doneness (160°F) or until center is no longer pink and juices show no pink color.

3 Cut meatloaf crosswise in half. Cut one half into 8 slices and serve. Tightly wrap remaining half; refrigerate up to 2 days for use in Southern BBQ Meatloaf Sandwiches.

Makes 4 servings (serving size: 2 slices).

Southern BBQ Meatloaf Sandwiches

½ **Favorite Family Meatloaf**

½ **cup prepared barbecue sauce**

1½ **teaspoons cider vinegar**

¼ **teaspoon pepper**

4 **onion rolls *or* hamburger buns, split**

½ **cup prepared creamy coleslaw**

Total preparation time: 15 minutes

1 In small bowl, combine barbecue sauce, vinegar and pepper; mix well.

2 Cut meatloaf into 8 slices. Place 2 slices on bottom half of each roll; top each with approximately 2 tablespoons sauce and 2 tablespoons coleslaw. Close sandwiches.

Makes 4 servings (serving size: 1 sandwich).

Cook's Tip

Meatloaf, wrapped tightly in aluminum foil, may be frozen up to 3 months; defrost in refrigerator before using.

Chili-Salsa Pot Roast

Beef & Spanish Rice Taco Salad

Chili-Salsa Pot Roast

3 to 3¼ - pound boneless beef chuck shoulder pot roast *or* bottom round roast

1 tablespoon vegetable oil

2 teaspoons chili powder

½ teaspoon salt

¼ teaspoon pepper

1 cup prepared thick and chunky salsa

½ cup water

1 medium yellow squash, cut into 1-inch pieces

1 medium zucchini, cut into 1-inch pieces

2 tablespoons cornstarch dissolved in 3 tablespoons water

Cook's Tip

Cooked pot roast, wrapped tightly in aluminum foil, may be frozen up to 3 months; defrost in refrigerator before using.

Total preparation & cooking time: 3½ hours

1 In Dutch oven, heat oil over medium heat until hot. Press chili powder evenly into surface of beef pot roast. Add pot roast; brown evenly. Pour off drippings. Season with salt and pepper.

2 Add salsa and water. Bring to a boil; reduce heat to low. Cover tightly and simmer gently 2¾ hours. Add vegetables. Cover tightly and continue simmering 15 minutes or until pot roast and vegetables are tender.

3 Remove pot roast and vegetables; keep warm. Skim fat from cooking liquid. In same pan, combine cooking liquid and cornstarch mixture. Bring to a boil; cook and stir 1 minute or until thickened. Set aside 1 cup sauce.

4 While still warm, cut pot roast in half. Trim and discard excess fat. Carve one portion into slices. Serve with vegetables and remaining sauce.

5 Shred remaining portion of beef with 2 forks to yield 3 to 3½ cups. Add 1 cup reserved sauce. Cover and refrigerate beef mixture up to 4 days for later use in Beef & Spanish Rice Taco Salad.

Makes 4 to 6 servings.

Beef & Spanish Rice Taco Salad

3 to 3½ cups shredded beef mixture from Chili-Salsa Pot Roast

1 package (5.6 ounces) flour tortilla salad shells (4 shells)

1 package (4.3 to 4.4 ounces) quick-cooking Spanish rice mix

2 cups thinly sliced lettuce

1 cup chopped tomato

1 cup (4 ounces) shredded Cheddar cheese

Toppings (optional)

Chopped avocado

Dairy sour cream

Chopped fresh cilantro

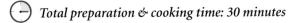 *Total preparation & cooking time: 30 minutes*

1 Prepare salad shells according to package directions. Prepare rice mix according to package directions.

2 In 1½-quart microwave-safe dish, place shredded beef mixture. Cover and microwave on HIGH 5 to 6 minutes or until hot; stir once.

3 Layer equal amounts of rice, lettuce, beef mixture, tomato and cheese into salad shells. Top with avocado, sour cream and cilantro, if desired.

Makes 4 servings.

Cook's Tips

One package (6.5 ounces) corn taco salad shells (8 shells) may be substituted for flour tortilla salad shells.

To reheat beef on stovetop, in medium saucepan, combine ingredients as stated in Step 2. Heat over medium heat 11 to 13 minutes or until hot; stir occasionally.

Company's Coming

Chapter 5

Whether company's coming for a casual weekend supper or a "pull out all the stops" holiday meal, this chapter has it covered. Many of these dishes can be on the table in an hour or less. All are guaranteed easy and company-perfect — whether you choose a stunning beef rib roast or a 30-minute beef Burgundy.

Herb-Crusted Beef Rib Roast,
Page 96

Beef Kabobs With Asian Noodles

1¼ pounds boneless beef
top sirloin steak, cut
1 inch thick

⅓ cup prepared Thai
peanut sauce

Asian Noodles

¼ cup rice wine vinegar

2 tablespoons vegetable
oil

4 teaspoons soy sauce

1½ teaspoons sugar

1 teaspoon grated fresh
ginger

4 ounces uncooked angel
hair pasta

1 cup thinly sliced halved
seedless cucumber

1 medium red bell pepper,
cut into 1½ x ⅛-inch
strips

🕐 *Total preparation & cooking time: 25 minutes*

1 In large bowl, whisk together vinegar, oil, soy
sauce, sugar and ginger until blended. Set aside.

2 Cook pasta according to package directions;
drain. Add pasta, cucumber and bell pepper to large
bowl; toss gently to coat.

3 Meanwhile cut beef steak into 1¼-inch pieces.
Thread equal amounts of beef onto each of four
10-inch metal skewers. Brush beef with half the
peanut sauce. Place kabobs on rack in broiler pan
so surface of beef is 3 to 4 inches from heat. Broil
8 to 10 minutes for medium rare to medium doneness; turn once and brush with remaining peanut
sauce halfway through cooking time.

4 Serve kabobs with Asian Noodles.

Makes 4 servings.

Cook's Tip

*Asian Noodles are served at room
temperature.*

Braised Beef With Roasted Vegetables

Cook's Tip

For chuck eye pot roast, tie at 2-inch intervals with heavy cotton string.

2½ to 3 - pound boneless beef chuck pot roast (arm, blade, chuck eye *or* shoulder)

2 teaspoons vegetable oil

½ teaspoon salt

¼ teaspoon pepper

1 can (13¾ to 14½ ounces) ready-to-serve beef broth

½ cup chopped onion

1 large clove garlic, crushed

2 tablespoons chopped fresh parsley

1 bay leaf

Roasted Vegetables

2 tablespoons cornstarch dissolved in 3 tablespoons water

Chopped fresh parsley (optional)

Total preparation & cooking time: 2 ¾ hours

1 In Dutch oven, heat oil over medium heat until hot. Add beef pot roast; brown evenly. Season with salt and pepper.

2 Add broth, onion, garlic, 2 tablespoons parsley and bay leaf. Bring to a boil; reduce heat to low. Cover tightly and simmer gently 2 ¼ to 2 ½ hours or until pot roast is tender.

3 Approximately 1 hour before end of cooking time, prepare Roasted Vegetables.

4 Remove pot roast; keep warm. Skim fat from cooking liquid; discard bay leaf. In same pan, combine 2 cups cooking liquid and cornstarch mixture. Bring to a boil; cook and stir 1 minute or until thickened.

5 Serve pot roast with vegetables and gravy. Garnish with chopped parsley, if desired.

Makes 6 to 8 servings.

Roasted Vegetables

8 small parsnips (approx. 1 pound), peeled

6 small leeks (approx. 2 pounds), well cleaned

2 red bell peppers, cut into 2-inch pieces

2 tablespoons vegetable oil

1½ teaspoons dried marjoram leaves, crushed

½ teaspoon salt

¼ teaspoon pepper

1 Heat oven to 350°F. Cut parsnips into 3-inch lengths; cut thick end pieces lengthwise in half. Cut leeks into 3-inch lengths (white and light green parts only). Place vegetables in 15 x 10-inch jelly-roll pan. Drizzle with oil; sprinkle with marjoram, salt and pepper. Toss to coat.

2 Roast in 350°F oven 40 to 50 minutes or until tender and lightly browned; stir once.

Makes 6 to 8 servings.

Cook's Note

To clean leeks, remove outer leaves and trim tops of leeks. Cut off roots; cut leeks lengthwise in half to within 1 inch of root ends. Separate leaves slightly. Hold leeks under cold running water to remove sand and grit.

Cook's Tip

Six medium carrots may be substituted for bell peppers. Peel and cut carrots the same as parsnips.

Mexican Beef Stew

3 pounds boneless beef round *or* chuck, cut into 1-inch pieces

2 tablespoons vegetable oil

½ teaspoon salt

1 cup ready-to-serve beef broth

1 cup prepared thick and chunky salsa

2 medium zucchini, halved lengthwise, then cut crosswise into ¾-inch-thick pieces

1 can (15 ounces) black beans, rinsed, drained

½ cup frozen whole corn kernels

2 tablespoons cornstarch dissolved in 3 tablespoons water

Toppings (optional)

Chopped fresh cilantro

Dairy sour cream

Chopped tomato

Total preparation & cooking time: 1¾ to 2 hours

1 In Dutch oven, heat oil over medium-high heat until hot. Cook and stir beef in 2 batches; brown evenly. Pour off drippings. Return beef to pan. Season with salt.

2 Stir in broth and salsa. Bring to a boil; reduce heat to low. Cover tightly and simmer gently 1¼ hours.

3 Stir in zucchini, beans and corn. Bring to a boil; reduce heat to low. Cover tightly and continue simmering 15 to 20 minutes or until beef and vegetables are tender.

4 Stir in cornstarch mixture. Bring to a boil; cook and stir 1 minute or until thickened. Serve with toppings, if desired.

Makes 6 to 8 servings (serving size: approx. 1 cup).

Cook's Note

Cooking beef in liquid (also called stewing) results in moist, fork-tender beef. Add enough liquid to cover the beef and simmer gently, tightly covered, without boiling.

Herb-Crusted Beef Rib Roast

Creamy Horseradish & Chive Sauce

In 1-quart bowl, combine 2 cups dairy sour cream, 1/2 cup prepared horseradish, 1/3 cup milk, 2 table-spoons snipped fresh chives and 1/4 teaspoon ground white pepper. Set aside 1 cup sauce for Horseradish-Stuffed Potatoes. Cover and refrigerate remaining sauce until ready to serve.

Makes approx. 2 3/4 cups.

6 to 8 - pound beef rib roast (2 to 4 ribs) small end, chine (back) bone removed

Creamy Horseradish & Chive Sauce *(see recipe at left)*

Horseradish-Stuffed Potatoes

Seasoning

2 tablespoons minced fresh parsley

1 tablespoon dried thyme leaves, crushed

1 tablespoon vegetable oil

2 teaspoons cracked black pepper

4 cloves garlic, crushed

Total preparation & cooking time: 2 3/4 to 3 1/2 hours

1 Prepare Creamy Horseradish & Chive Sauce and Horseradish-Stuffed Potatoes the day before.

2 Heat oven to 350°F. In small bowl, combine seasoning ingredients. Press evenly into surface of beef roast.

3 Place roast, fat-side up, in shallow roasting pan. Insert ovenproof meat thermometer so tip is centered in thickest part, not resting in fat or touching bone. Do not add water or cover. Roast 2 1/4 to 2 1/2 hours for medium rare; 2 3/4 to 3 hours for medium doneness.

4 About 45 minutes before roast is done, bake stuffed potatoes.

5 Remove roast when meat thermometer registers 135°F for medium rare; 150°F for medium doneness. Transfer roast to carving board; tent loosely with aluminum foil. Let stand 15 minutes. (Temperature will continue to rise approximately 10°F to reach 145°F for medium rare; 160°F for medium.)

6 Carve roast. Serve with horseradish sauce and potatoes.

Makes 8 to 10 servings.

Horseradish-Stuffed Potatoes

8 baking potatoes (approx. 8 ounces *each*)

1 teaspoon salt

¼ teaspoon ground white pepper

1 cup Creamy Horseradish & Chive Sauce

¼ cup butter, softened

¼ cup diced red bell pepper

Garnishes (optional)

1 tablespoon snipped fresh chives

1 tablespoon diced red bell pepper

Total preparation & cooking time: 2 ¼ hours
Chilling time: overnight

1 The day before roasting Herb-Crusted Beef Rib Roast, heat oven to 400°F. Pierce potatoes several times with fork. Place potatoes on oven rack. Bake in 400°F oven 60 minutes or until cooked through and tender. Cool 5 minutes.

2 Cut top ⅓ from potatoes; remove potato pulp from top to large bowl. Scoop potato pulp from bottoms, leaving ¼-inch-thick shell.

3 Mash potato pulp. Season with salt and pepper. Add Creamy Horseradish & Chive Sauce, butter and ¼ cup bell pepper; stir to combine. Spoon potato mixture back into potato shells. Place on baking sheet. Cover and refrigerate overnight.

4 Heat oven to 350°F. Remove potatoes from refrigerator. Bake in 350°F oven 45 minutes or until heated through and lightly browned.

5 Garnish with chives and 1 tablespoon bell pepper, if desired.

Makes 8 stuffed potatoes (serving size: 1 potato).

Cook's Note

Prepared horseradish, found in the refrigerated case in the supermarket, is grated horseradish root, usually with vinegar added to stabilize the heat. Refrigerate it at home to retain the zesty, fresh flavor.

Four-Pepper Beef Tenderloin

2- pound beef tenderloin
   roast, center cut

Seasoning

  1 teaspoon dried oregano
    leaves, crushed

  1 teaspoon sweet paprika

  1 teaspoon salt

  1 teaspoon dried thyme
    leaves, crushed

  ½ teaspoon garlic powder

  ½ teaspoon ground black
    pepper

  ½ teaspoon onion powder

  ¼ teaspoon ground red
    pepper

  ¼ teaspoon ground white
    pepper

Total preparation & cooking time: 1 hour

1 Heat oven to 425°F. In small bowl, combine seasoning ingredients. Press evenly into surface of beef roast.

2 Place roast on rack in shallow roasting pan. Insert ovenproof meat thermometer so tip is centered in thickest part of beef. Do not add water or cover. Roast in 425°F oven 35 to 40 minutes for medium rare doneness. Remove roast when meat thermometer registers 135°F. Transfer roast to carving board; tent loosely with aluminum foil. Let stand 15 minutes. (Temperature will continue to rise approximately 10°F to reach 145°F for medium rare.)

3 Carve roast into ½-inch-thick slices.

Makes 6 servings.

Cook's Notes

Paprika is a powder made by grinding sweet red pepper pods. The flavor can range from mild to hot and the color is bright orange-red to red.

A center-cut beef tenderloin roast is cut from the center portion of the whole tenderloin. The center cut is uniform in size, ensuring even cooking throughout.

Savory Carrots & Prunes

*In medium saucepan, combine
1 cup ready-to-serve beef broth,
1/3 cup packed brown sugar,
1 tablespoon fresh lemon juice
and 1/2 teaspoon ground cinna-
mon. Cook and stir over medium
heat until sugar is dissolved. Stir
in 1 package (16 ounces) fresh
baby carrots. Bring to a boil;
reduce heat to low. Cover tightly
and simmer 10 minutes or until
carrots are crisp-tender. Stir in
1 cup pitted prunes; increase
heat to medium-high. Cook,
uncovered, 5 minutes or until
liquid is reduced and prunes
are plump; stir occasionally.*

Makes 6 to 8 servings.

Beef Brisket With Horseradish Sauce

**4 to 4 1/2 - pound fresh beef
brisket (first cut, flat half),
trimmed**

1 tablespoon vegetable oil

**2 medium onions, thinly
sliced**

**3/4 cup ready-to-serve beef
broth**

2 cloves garlic, crushed

**Savory Carrots & Prunes
(see recipe at left)**

**1 to 2 tablespoons prepared
horseradish**

Total preparation & cooking time: 3 1/4 to 3 3/4 hours

1 In Dutch oven or deep large skillet, heat oil over
medium heat until hot. Add beef brisket; brown
evenly. Remove brisket from pan.

2 Add onions to same pan. Cook and stir 3 minutes
or until crisp-tender. Pour off drippings. Add brisket,
broth and garlic. Bring to a boil; reduce heat to low.
Cover tightly and simmer gently 3 to 3 1/2 hours or
until brisket is tender. Remove brisket; keep warm.

3 Meanwhile prepare Savory Carrots & Prunes.

4 Skim fat from pan juices. Cook pan juices,
uncovered, over medium-high heat 5 minutes or
until reduced by half; stir in horseradish. Carve
brisket diagonally across the grain into thin slices.
Serve with sauce and Savory Carrots & Prunes.

Makes 6 to 8 servings.

Quick Beef Burgundy

1 package fully cooked, ready-to-heat-and-eat boneless beef pot roast (1¾ to 2½ pounds)

10 ounces uncooked egg noodles

1 pound small mushrooms

2 small onions, cut into thin wedges, separated

⅔ cup Burgundy *or* dry red wine

¾ teaspoon dried marjoram leaves, crushed

1 tablespoon cornstarch dissolved in 3 tablespoons water

Chopped fresh parsley (optional)

Total preparation & cooking time: 30 minutes

1 Cook noodles according to package directions; drain and keep warm.

2 Meanwhile remove pot roast from package; transfer liquid to Dutch oven. Cut pot roast into 1-inch pieces; set aside.

3 Add mushrooms, onions, wine and marjoram to liquid. Bring to a boil; reduce heat to medium-low. Simmer, uncovered, 7 to 8 minutes or until vegetables are almost tender; stir occasionally.

4 Add beef. Bring to a boil. Cook 2 to 3 minutes or until beef is heated through; stir occasionally. Stir in cornstarch mixture. Bring to a boil; cook and stir 1 minute or until thickened. Serve over noodles; sprinkle with parsley, if desired.

Makes 4 servings.

Cook's Note

Look for fully cooked, ready-to-heat-and-eat boneless beef pot roasts with natural juices in the meat department of your supermarket. They range from 1¾ to 2½ pounds and need only a quick heating in the microwave oven before serving.

Crumb-Crusted Dijon Sirloin

2-pound boneless beef top sirloin steak, cut 1½ inches thick

1 teaspoon olive oil

2 tablespoons Dijon-style mustard

1 clove garlic, crushed

¼ teaspoon pepper

½ cup soft bread crumbs

¼ cup chopped fresh parsley

Baked Potato Wedges

4 medium baking potatoes (approx. 2 pounds), *each* cut lengthwise into 8 wedges

2 tablespoons olive oil

1 clove garlic, crushed

½ teaspoon salt

¼ teaspoon pepper

2 tablespoons chopped fresh parsley

Total preparation & cooking time: 1½ hours

1 Heat oven to 350°F. Place potatoes in 15 x 10-inch jelly-roll pan. In small bowl, combine 2 tablespoons oil, 1 clove garlic, salt and ¼ teaspoon pepper. Drizzle over potatoes; toss to coat. Spread potatoes in single layer. Bake in 350°F oven 20 minutes.

2 Meanwhile in large nonstick skillet, heat 1 teaspoon oil over medium-high heat until hot. Add steak to skillet; brown on both sides. Place steak on rack in shallow roasting pan. In small bowl, combine mustard, 1 clove garlic and ¼ teaspoon pepper; spread on top of steak. In another bowl, toss bread crumbs with ¼ cup parsley; pat evenly over mustard mixture.

3 After potatoes have baked 20 minutes, place steak in same 350°F oven. Bake 35 to 40 minutes for medium rare to medium doneness. Remove steak when meat thermometer registers 140°F for medium rare; 155°F for medium. Transfer steak to carving board. Let stand 5 minutes. (Temperature will continue to rise 5°F to 145°F for medium rare; 160°F for medium.) Continue baking potatoes 5 minutes or until tender.

4 Carve steak. Sprinkle potatoes with parsley.

Makes 6 servings.

Cook's Note

To accurately determine steak doneness, use an instant-read thermometer to check the internal temperature. Refer to pages 16 and 17 for more information on thermometers and determining doneness.

Grilled Beef & Smoked Gouda Pizzas

1¼ - **pound boneless beef top sirloin steak, cut ¾ inch thick**

2 **tablespoons cornmeal**

2 **packages (10 ounces** *each*) **refrigerated pizza dough**

3 **tablespoons olive oil**

1 **small eggplant (6 to 7 inches long), cut crosswise into ½-inch-thick slices**

1 **large yellow bell pepper, quartered**

2 **teaspoons lemon pepper**

2 **medium plum tomatoes, very thinly sliced**

1 **cup (4 ounces) shredded smoked Gouda cheese**

Cook's Note

Smoked Gouda cheese has a mild, smoky, slightly nutty flavor and creamy texture.

Total preparation & cooking time: 1½ hours

1 Sprinkle cornmeal on 2 large baking sheets. Unroll each pizza dough and cut in half. Place 2 halves on each baking sheet. Press each piece into approximately 8 x 5-inch free-form rectangle; brush lightly with some of the oil. Cover with plastic wrap and refrigerate.

2 Brush eggplant and bell pepper with oil. Press lemon pepper evenly into both sides of beef steak. Place steak on grid over medium, ash-covered coals; arrange eggplant and bell pepper around steak. Grill, uncovered, 13 to 16 minutes or until steak is medium rare to medium doneness and vegetables are tender; turn occasionally. Brush eggplant with any remaining oil during grilling, if needed. Remove steak and vegetables from grill; cool slightly. Allow coals to cool to medium-low.

3 Carefully place pizza crusts, cornmeal-side down, directly on grid over medium-low coals. (If necessary, crusts can be grilled in 2 batches.) Grill, uncovered, 3 to 4 minutes or until edges are puffy and bottoms have brown grill marks. (Watch carefully so that crusts do not burn.) Turn crusts over. Grill second side 1 minute or until partially cooked. Return crusts to baking sheets, cornmeal-coated sides up.

4 Cut eggplant slices into quarters. Cut bell pepper pieces into thin strips. Carve steak crosswise into thin slices. Arrange equal amounts of eggplant, tomatoes, beef and bell pepper on pizza crusts; sprinkle with cheese.

5 Grill, covered, over medium-low coals 2 to 3 minutes or until crusts are cooked and browned on bottom, and cheese is softened. (Cheese does not melt completely.) Watch carefully so that crusts do not burn; rotate pizzas as necessary.

Makes 4 servings (serving size: 1 pizza).

Beef & Wild Mushroom Lasagna

1 pound 80% lean ground beef

2 tablespoons olive oil

1 pound assorted wild mushrooms (such as shiitake, oyster and cremini), sliced

¼ teaspoon salt

1 jar (approx. 26 ounces) prepared roasted garlic *or* roasted garlic and onion spaghetti sauce

1 can (14½ ounces) diced tomatoes with basil, garlic and oregano, undrained

1 carton (15 ounces) part-skim ricotta cheese

1 egg, slightly beaten

10 uncooked lasagna noodles (not oven-ready)

4 cups (16 ounces) shredded pizza cheese blend

Total preparation & cooking time: 1¼ hours
Standing time: 15 minutes

1 Heat oven to 375°F. In large nonstick skillet, heat oil over medium heat until hot. Add mushrooms. Cook and stir 4 to 6 minutes or until tender.

2 In same skillet, brown ground beef over medium heat 6 minutes or until outside surface is no longer pink, breaking up into ¾-inch crumbles. Pour off drippings. Season with salt. Stir in spaghetti sauce and tomatoes.

3 In medium bowl, combine ricotta cheese and egg.

4 Spread 2 cups beef sauce in 13 x 9-inch baking dish. Place 4 noodles lengthwise and 1 noodle crosswise (break to fit) in a single layer; press lightly. Spread ricotta mixture evenly over noodles; top with mushrooms. Sprinkle with 2 cups shredded cheese. Spread 2½ cups sauce over cheese. Cover with remaining noodles; press lightly into sauce. Spread remaining sauce over noodles.

5 Bake, uncovered, 45 to 50 minutes or until noodles are tender. Sprinkle with remaining cheese. Tent lightly with aluminum foil; let stand 15 minutes before cutting.

Makes 9 servings.

Cook's Tips

Wild mushrooms are varieties other than the typical white button mushroom including cremini, oyster and shiitake. These mushrooms once grew only wild, but now they are also grown commercially.

Recipe may be made with only cremini mushrooms, if desired.

Curry Beef Stir-Fry With Sugar Snap Peas

1¼-pound high-quality beef top round steak, cut 1 inch thick

1 tablespoon vegetable oil

1½ cups fresh sugar snap peas

1 medium onion, cut into thin wedges

1 teaspoon hot curry powder

½ teaspoon salt

½ cup canned unsweetened coconut milk

2 cups hot cooked rice

Toasted sliced almonds (optional)

Marinade

¼ cup water

2 tablespoons grated fresh ginger

1 tablespoon hot curry powder

1 tablespoon vegetable oil

2 cloves garlic, crushed

Total preparation & cooking time: 35 minutes
Marinating time: 1 to 2 hours

1 In small bowl, combine marinade ingredients. Cut beef steak lengthwise in half, then crosswise into ⅛-inch-thick strips. Place beef and marinade in food-safe plastic bag; turn to coat. Close bag securely. Marinate in refrigerator 1 to 2 hours; turn occasionally.

2 In large nonstick skillet, heat 1 tablespoon oil over medium heat until hot. Add sugar snap peas, onion and 1 teaspoon curry powder. Stir-fry 7 to 8 minutes or until vegetables are crisp-tender. Remove from skillet.

3 Remove beef from marinade; discard marinade. Heat same skillet over medium-high heat until hot. Stir-fry beef and marinade in 2 batches, 1 to 2 minutes each, or until outside surface is no longer pink. (Do not overcook.) Return beef to skillet. Season with salt. Add vegetables; stir in coconut milk. Continue cooking 1 to 2 minutes or until just heated through.

4 Serve over rice. Sprinkle with almonds, if desired.

Makes 4 servings.

Cook's Note

Unsweetened coconut milk is a combination of water and coconut meat that has been simmered and strained. It is available canned in the ethnic section of the supermarket.

Cook's Tip

One package (9 ounces) frozen sugar snap peas may be substituted for fresh sugar snap peas.

Hot Off The Grill

Chapter 6

Beef and grilling are natural partners and these recipes are the best of the best. Marvelous marinades, robust rubs, sumptuous stuffings — you'll find them here. There's a great grilled beef choice for every occasion.

Steak Soft Tacos, Page 135

Pacific Rim-Glazed Steak

1½ to 2-pound beef
flank steak

Marinade

1 cup prepared teriyaki
marinade and sauce

½ cup chopped onion

⅓ cup honey

⅓ cup fresh orange juice

1 tablespoon chopped
fresh rosemary

1 tablespoon dark sesame
oil

1 large clove garlic, crushed

Pepper

Garnishes (optional)

Orange slices

Rosemary sprigs

Total preparation & cooking time: 25 minutes
Marinating time: 30 minutes

1 In small bowl, combine marinade ingredients; add pepper, as desired. Set aside ¾ cup marinade for basting.

2 Place steak and remaining marinade in food-safe plastic bag; turn to coat. Close bag securely and marinate in refrigerator 30 minutes; turn once.

3 Remove steak from marinade; discard marinade. Place steak on grid over medium, ash-covered coals. Grill, uncovered, 17 to 21 minutes for medium rare to medium doneness; turn occasionally and baste with reserved ¾ cup marinade.

4 Place remaining basting marinade in small saucepan; place on grid of grill and bring to a boil. Meanwhile carve steak diagonally across the grain into thin slices. Spoon hot marinade over beef. Garnish with orange slices and rosemary sprigs, if desired.

Makes 6 to 8 servings.

1997 National Beef Cook-Off ®
★ *Best of Beef Winner* ★

Grilled Steak & Colorful Peppers

2 beef Porterhouse *or* T-Bone steaks, cut 1 inch thick (approx. 1 pound *each*)

2 small red, yellow *or* green bell peppers, quartered

Salt

Pepper

Parsley Pesto

½ cup packed Italian parsley leaves

4 large cloves garlic, crushed

3 tablespoons olive oil

Cook's Tip

A Porterhouse steak differs from a T-Bone in that the Porterhouse tenderloin diameter is no less than 1¼ inches measured across the center compared to the T-Bone tenderloin, which is not less than ½ inch.

Total preparation & cooking time: 30 minutes

1 In small bowl of food processor fitted with steel blade, combine pesto ingredients. Cover and process until parsley is finely chopped; scrape bowl frequently.

2 Generously spread pesto on both sides of beef steaks and peppers. Place on grid over medium, ash-covered coals. Grill, uncovered, 14 to 16 minutes or until steaks are medium rare to medium doneness and peppers are tender; turn occasionally.

3 Remove bone; carve steak crosswise into slices. Season with salt and pepper, as desired.

Makes 4 servings.

Cook's Note

Approximately 30 minutes prior to grilling, prepare the charcoal fire so coals have time to reach medium temperature. At medium, the coals will be ash-covered. To check the temperature of the coals, spread the coals in a single layer. Carefully hold the palm of your hand above the coals at cooking height. Count the number of seconds you can hold your hand in that position before the heat forces you to pull it away; approximately 4 seconds for medium heat. Position the cooking grid and follow recipe directions.

For gas grills, consult the owner's manual for preheating instructions.

Star-Spangled Cheeseburgers

2 **pounds 80% lean ground beef**

Salt

Pepper

BBQ Ketchup Spread *or* Honey-Mustard Spread *(recipes follow)*

8 **slices (approx. 1 ounce *each*) American cheese**

8 **hamburger buns, split**

Romaine lettuce

Tomato slices

BBQ Ketchup Spread

In a small bowl, combine ¼ cup ketchup and 2 tablespoons prepared barbecue sauce.

Makes approx. ⅓ cup.

Honey-Mustard Spread

In a small bowl, combine ¼ cup mayonnaise and ¼ cup prepared honey mustard.

Makes approx. ½ cup.

Total preparation & cooking time: 30 minutes

1 Shape ground beef into eight ½-inch-thick patties.

2 Place patties on grid over medium, ash-covered coals. Grill, uncovered, 11 to 13 minutes to medium doneness (160°F) or until centers are no longer pink and juices show no pink color; turn once. Season with salt and pepper, as desired.

3 Meanwhile prepare BBQ Ketchup Spread or Honey-Mustard Spread. Cut shapes from cheese slices, using star-shaped cookie cutter.

4 Approximately 1 minute before burgers are done, place cheese stars on top of burgers.

5 Spread cut surfaces of buns with desired spread. Place lettuce and tomato on bottom of each bun, as desired. Top with burger. Close sandwiches.

Makes 8 servings (serving size: 1 sandwich).

Cook's Note

Use a gentle touch when shaping ground beef patties. Overhandling will result in a firm compact texture after cooking. Don't press or flatten with spatula during cooking.

Spicy Ribeyes With Grilled Sweet Onions

4 beef ribeye steaks, cut
  1 inch thick (approx.
  8 ounces *each*)

2 large (14 to 16 ounces
  each) sweet onions, cut
  into ½-inch slices

2 tablespoons olive oil

½ teaspoon salt

¼ teaspoon pepper

1 lime, quartered

Seasoning

1 teaspoon garlic powder

½ teaspoon ground cumin

½ teaspoon dried oregano
  leaves, crushed

¼ teaspoon ground red
  pepper

½ teaspoon salt

Total preparation & cooking time: 20 minutes

1 In small bowl, combine seasoning ingredients. Press evenly into both sides of each beef steak.

2 Brush onions with oil. Place onions on grid over medium, ash-covered coals. Grill, uncovered, 15 to 20 minutes or until tender; turn once. Grill steaks 11 to 14 minutes for medium rare to medium doneness; turn once. Season onions with salt and pepper.

3 Squeeze lime over steaks and onions.

Makes 4 servings.

Cook's Note

Sweet onions are the onion varieties such as Vidalia, Walla Walla and Imperial Sweets that are considered to be exceptionally sweet and juicy.

117

Sizzling Summer Steak

2-pound high-quality beef top round steak, cut 1½ inches thick

Marinade

½ cup fresh lime juice

3 tablespoons minced green onions

3 tablespoons water

2 tablespoons vegetable oil

1 tablespoon minced fresh ginger

3 large cloves garlic, crushed

½ teaspoon salt

Total preparation & cooking time: 35 minutes
Marinating time: 6 to 8 hours or overnight

1 In small bowl, combine marinade ingredients. Place beef steak and marinade in food-safe plastic bag; turn to coat. Close bag securely and marinate in refrigerator 6 to 8 hours or overnight; turn occasionally.

2 Remove steak from marinade; discard marinade. Place steak on grid over medium, ash-covered coals. Grill, covered, 25 to 28 minutes to 140°F for medium rare doneness; turn occasionally. Transfer to carving board. Let stand 5 minutes. (Temperature will continue to rise 5°F to reach 145°F for medium rare.) Carve steak crosswise into thin slices.

Makes 6 to 8 servings.

Cook's Note

Ginger is a bumpy, knobby root with peppery, sweet flavor. The skin is removed and the ivory colored flesh is grated, slivered, chopped or minced. It's especially popular in Asian and Indian cooking. Also, fresh ginger contains a natural tenderizing enzyme that when used in marinades helps tenderize less tender beef cuts.

Cook's Tip

Do not substitute powdered ginger for the fresh; it does not have the natural tenderizing enzyme found in fresh ginger.

Grilled Steaks With Tomato & Pesto Pasta

Cook's Tip

Tomato & Pesto Pasta is served at room temperature.

4 boneless beef top loin steaks, cut 1 inch thick (approx. 8 ounces *each*)

2 teaspoons freshly grated lemon peel

1 teaspoon coarse grind black pepper

8 teaspoons prepared basil pesto sauce

Lemon slices (optional)

Tomato & Pesto Pasta

3 cups uncooked rotini pasta

2 medium tomatoes, chopped

$\frac{1}{3}$ cup chopped fresh basil

$\frac{1}{4}$ cup prepared basil pesto sauce

2 teaspoons freshly grated lemon peel

🕐 *Total preparation & cooking time: 30 minutes*

1 Combine 2 teaspoons lemon peel and pepper. Press evenly into both sides of each beef steak. Place steaks on grid over medium, ash-covered coals. Grill, uncovered, 15 to 18 minutes for medium rare to medium doneness; turn occasionally.

2 Meanwhile cook pasta according to package directions; drain. In large bowl, combine pasta with remaining Tomato & Pesto Pasta ingredients.

3 Top each steak with 2 teaspoons basil pesto sauce. Serve with Tomato & Pesto Pasta. Garnish with lemon slices, if desired.

Makes 4 servings.

Balsamic-Marinated Sirloin & Asparagus

1¼-pound boneless beef top sirloin steak, cut 1 inch thick

1 pound fresh asparagus, trimmed

½ teaspoon salt

⅛ teaspoon pepper

Balsamic Marinade

¼ cup balsamic vinegar

2 tablespoons olive oil

1 tablespoon chopped fresh basil

1½ teaspoons Dijon-style mustard

1 clove garlic, crushed

½ teaspoon sugar

Total preparation & cooking time: 30 minutes
Marinating time: 15 minutes to 2 hours

1 In small bowl, combine marinade ingredients. Place beef steak and ⅓ cup marinade in food-safe plastic bag; turn to coat. Close bag securely and marinate in refrigerator 15 minutes to 2 hours; turn occasionally. Cover and refrigerate remaining marinade.

2 Meanwhile in large skillet, bring 1 inch of water to a boil; add asparagus. Reduce heat to medium-low. Cover and cook 2 to 3 minutes or until crisp-tender. Drain. In shallow dish, combine asparagus and reserved marinade; turn to coat. Set aside.

3 Remove steak from marinade; discard marinade. Place steak on grid over medium, ash-covered coals. Grill, uncovered, 17 to 21 minutes for medium rare to medium doneness; turn occasionally. During last 3 minutes of grilling, arrange asparagus on grid around steak. Grill 3 minutes; turn once.

4 Season steak and asparagus with salt and pepper. Carve steak crosswise into slices; serve with asparagus.

Makes 4 servings.

Cook's Tip

To microwave asparagus, place asparagus and ½ cup water in shallow microwave-safe dish; cover. Microwave on HIGH 5 to 6 minutes or until crisp-tender. Drain.

Rosemary-Pepper Beef With Steak Fries

4 boneless beef top loin steaks, cut 1 inch thick (approx. 8 ounces *each*)

½ bag (14 ounces) frozen steak fries

Salt

Seasoning

1 tablespoon olive oil

2 teaspoons finely chopped fresh rosemary

2 large cloves garlic, crushed

¾ teaspoon coarse grind black pepper

Total preparation & cooking time: 25 minutes

1 In large bowl, combine seasoning ingredients. Remove approximately 2 teaspoons seasoning mixture; press evenly into both sides of each beef steak.

2 Add potatoes to remaining seasoning mixture in bowl; toss to coat.

3 Place steaks in center of grid over medium, ash-covered coals. Arrange potatoes around steaks. Grill, uncovered, 15 to 18 minutes for medium rare to medium doneness; turn steaks and potatoes occasionally.

4 Season potatoes with salt, as desired. Serve with steaks.

Makes 4 servings.

Cook's Notes

Arrange the potatoes around the outermost portion of the grill, where the coals are slightly cooler. Since the potatoes are precooked, they need only heating through.

Perishable foods should be consumed within two hours of preparation, one hour if outside in temperatures above 90°F.

Grilled Garlic-Stuffed Steaks

2 boneless beef top loin
steaks, cut 2 inches thick
(approx. 1 pound *each*)

1 tablespoon olive oil

¼ cup very finely chopped
garlic

½ cup thinly sliced green
onions

¼ teaspoon salt

¼ teaspoon pepper

Total preparation & cooking time: 45 minutes

1 In small nonstick skillet, heat oil over medium-low heat until hot. Add garlic. Cook and stir 4 to 5 minutes or until tender, but not browned. Add onions. Continue cooking and stirring 4 to 5 minutes or until onions are tender. Season with salt and pepper; cool completely.

2 Meanwhile with sharp knife, cut a pocket in each beef steak. *(See illustration, right.)* Start ½ inch from one long side of steak and cut horizontally through center of steak to within ½ inch of each side. Spread half of garlic mixture inside each steak pocket. Secure openings with wooden toothpicks.

3 Place steaks on grid over medium, ash-covered coals. Grill, covered, 22 to 24 minutes for medium rare to medium doneness; turn occasionally. Remove wooden toothpicks. Carve steaks crosswise into ½-inch-thick slices.

Makes 6 servings.

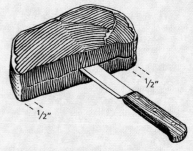

Cook's Tip

To cut pocket, start ½ inch from one long side of steak and cut horizontally through center of steak to within ½ inch of each side. Spread half of garlic mixture inside each steak pocket. Secure openings with wooden toothpicks.

Citrus-Ginger Beef Teriyaki

4 boneless beef chuck top blade steaks, cut ¾ to 1 inch thick (approx. 6 ounces *each*)

½ cup water

Toasted sesame seeds *or* diagonally sliced green onions (optional)

Marinade

½ cup prepared teriyaki marinade and sauce

⅓ cup orange marmalade

2 tablespoons creamy peanut butter

3 large cloves garlic, crushed

1 tablespoon finely chopped fresh ginger

2 teaspoons dark sesame oil

Total preparation & cooking time: 35 minutes
Marinating time: 30 minutes

1 In small saucepan, combine marinade ingredients. Heat over medium heat until slightly melted. Place beef steaks and ⅓ cup of marinade in food-safe plastic bag; turn to coat. Close bag securely and marinate in refrigerator 30 minutes; turn once. Set aside remaining marinade.

2 Remove steaks from marinade; discard marinade. Place steaks on grid over medium, ash-covered coals. Grill, uncovered, 16 to 20 minutes for medium rare to medium doneness; turn occasionally.

3 Meanwhile to make sauce, add water to reserved marinade in pan. Bring to a boil; reduce heat to low. Simmer, uncovered, 12 to 15 minutes or until slightly thickened; stir occasionally.

4 Serve steaks with sauce. Sprinkle with sesame seeds, if desired.

Makes 4 servings.

Cook's Notes

Teriyaki marinade and sauce is a prepared sauce (especially popular in Japanese cooking) usually made of soy sauce, ginger, sugar and seasonings that is used both to season foods and as an accompaniment. Look for it in the ethnic section of the supermarket.

Dark sesame oil is expressed from toasted sesame seeds; it has a strong sesame flavor and fragrance and is used predominantly as a flavor accent in sauces, dressings, marinades, etc.

Italian-Stuffed Burgers

1½ **pounds 80% lean ground beef**

½ **cup (2 ounces) shredded mozzarella cheese**

1 **can (4¼ ounces) chopped pitted ripe olives**

¼ **cup finely chopped onion**

Salt

4 **crusty rolls *or* hamburger buns, split, toasted**

4 **large tomato slices**

Seasoning

1 **tablespoon Italian seasoning, crushed**

1½ **teaspoons garlic powder**

½ **teaspoon pepper**

Toppings (optional)

Prepared pizza sauce

Mayonnaise

Thinly sliced lettuce

Total preparation & cooking time: 50 minutes

1 In small bowl, combine cheese, olives and onion. Shape ground beef into eight patties, approximately 4½-inch diameter. Place approximately ¼ cup of cheese mixture in center of four patties; top with remaining patties. Press edges firmly together to seal; gently pat to ¾-inch thickness.

2 In small bowl, combine seasoning ingredients. Press evenly into both sides of each patty.

3 Place patties on grid over medium, ash-covered coals. Grill, uncovered, 22 to 24 minutes to medium doneness (160°F) or until centers of patties are no longer pink and juices show no pink color; turn occasionally.

4 Season burgers with salt, as desired. Line bottom of each roll with one tomato slice; top with burger. Add choice of toppings, if desired. Close sandwiches.

Makes 4 servings (serving size: 1 sandwich).

Grilled Beef Quesadillas

¾ **pound thinly sliced deli roast beef**

1½ **cups prepared thick and chunky salsa**

¼ **cup chopped fresh cilantro**

3 **tablespoons fresh lime juice**

1 **cup canned black beans, rinsed, drained**

½ **cup frozen whole corn kernels, defrosted**

8 **small flour tortillas**

3 **cups (12 ounces) shredded Co-Jack cheese**

🕐 *Total preparation & cooking time: 25 minutes*

1 In medium bowl, combine salsa, cilantro and lime juice. In second bowl, combine ½ cup salsa mixture, beans and corn. Set aside remaining salsa mixture.

2 Sprinkle cheese evenly on one side of each tortilla; divide beef evenly among tortillas. Top with scant ¼ cup of bean mixture. Fold tortillas in half.

3 Place quesadillas on grid over medium, ash-covered coals. Grill, uncovered, 4 to 5 minutes or until golden brown; turn once. Serve with reserved salsa mixture.

Makes 4 servings (serving size: 2 quesadillas).

Cook's Tips

If black beans are large, slightly mash before adding to salsa mixture.

To serve as an appetizer or snack: cut each quesadilla into 3 wedges.

Steak Salad With Ranch Dressing

1¼-pound boneless beef
   top sirloin steak, cut
   ¾ inch thick

Salt

1 teaspoon fresh lemon
   juice

6 cups mesclun gourmet
   salad mix

2 medium plum tomatoes,
   halved lengthwise, then
   cut crosswise into slices

½ cup prepared peppercorn
   ranch dressing

Seasoning

1 teaspoon dried oregano
   leaves, crushed

1 clove garlic, crushed

¼ teaspoon pepper

Total preparation & cooking time: 25 minutes

1 In small bowl, combine seasoning ingredients. Press evenly into both sides of beef steak. Place steak on grid over medium, ash-covered coals. Grill, uncovered, 13 to 16 minutes for medium rare to medium doneness; turn occasionally.

2 Season steak with salt, as desired. Drizzle with lemon juice. Carve steak crosswise into thin slices.

3 In large bowl, combine salad mix and tomatoes; toss gently. Arrange beef on top of salad. Serve with dressing.

Makes 4 servings.

Cook's Note

Mesclun is a combination of young greens such as arugula, dandelion, frisée, mizuna, oak leaf, mâche, radicchio and sorrel.

Cook's Tip

Six cups of your favorite mixed greens may be substituted for the mesclun.

Island Jerk Beef & Pineapple Kabobs

Jerk Rub

In a small bowl, combine ¼ cup finely chopped green onions, 4 crushed large cloves garlic, 1 finely chopped jalapeño pepper, 1 tablespoon finely chopped fresh ginger, 1 tablespoon fresh lime juice, 2 teaspoons packed brown sugar, 1½ teaspoons dried thyme leaves, crushed, 1¼ teaspoons salt and ¾ teaspoon ground allspice.

Makes approx. ½ cup.

4 **boneless beef chuck eye steaks, cut ¾ to 1 inch thick (6 to 8 ounces** *each*)

Jerk Rub *(see recipe at left)*

Kabobs

½ **fresh pineapple, rind removed, cored, cut into 1 to 1½-inch pieces (approx. 1¼ pounds)**

3 **green onions, cut into 1½-inch-long pieces**

2 **tablespoons butter, melted**

2 **teaspoons packed brown sugar**

Dash ground red pepper

Cook's Tip

For a rub with less heat, seed jalapeño peppers before chopping.

Total preparation & cooking time: 1 hour

1 Prepare Jerk Rub.

2 Soak four 12-inch bamboo skewers in water 10 minutes; drain. Alternately thread pineapple and green onion pieces onto each skewer.

3 In small bowl, combine butter, brown sugar and red pepper.

4 Press Jerk Rub into both sides of each beef steak. Place steaks on grid over medium, ash-covered coals. Grill, uncovered, 14 to 18 minutes for medium rare to medium doneness; turn occasionally. Grill kabobs 8 to 10 minutes or until lightly browned; turn occasionally and brush with butter mixture during the last 5 minutes of grilling.

Makes 4 servings.

Grilled Steak Santa Fe

1¼-pound high-quality beef
    top round steak, cut
    1 inch thick

1 large avocado, diced

½ cup chopped red onion

Marinade

6 tablespoons frozen
    margarita drink mix
    concentrate, defrosted

2 tablespoons chopped
    fresh cilantro

2 tablespoons vegetable oil

4 cloves garlic, crushed

2 teaspoons ground cumin

½ teaspoon salt

¼ teaspoon pepper

Total preparation & cooking time: 40 minutes
Marinating time: 6 to 8 hours or overnight

1 In small bowl, combine marinade ingredients. Set aside 2 tablespoons of marinade; cover and refrigerate. Place beef steak and remaining marinade in food-safe plastic bag; turn to coat. Close bag securely and marinate in refrigerator 6 to 8 hours or overnight; turn occasionally.

2 Remove steak from marinade; discard marinade. Place steak on grid over medium, ash-covered coals. Grill, uncovered, 16 to 18 minutes for medium rare doneness; turn occasionally. Remove steak; keep warm.

3 Just before serving, in medium bowl, combine avocado, onion and reserved 2 tablespoons marinade; toss gently to coat.

4 Carve steak crosswise into thin slices. Serve immediately with avocado mixture.

Makes 4 servings.

Steak Soft Tacos

2 boneless beef chuck shoulder steaks, cut ¾ to 1 inch thick (approx. 12 ounces *each*)

Salt

12 small flour tortillas, warmed

Marinade

⅔ cup prepared Italian dressing

2 tablespoons coarsely chopped fresh cilantro

1 tablespoon chili powder

Toppings (optional)

Thinly sliced lettuce

Chopped tomato

Sour cream

Guacamole

Total preparation & cooking time: 20 minutes
Marinating time: 30 minutes to 6 hours.

1 In small bowl, combine marinade ingredients. Place beef steaks and marinade in food-safe plastic bag; turn to coat. Close bag securely and marinate in refrigerator 30 minutes to 6 hours; turn occasionally.

2 Remove steaks from marinade; discard marinade. Place steaks on grid over medium, ash-covered coals. Grill, uncovered, 14 to 18 minutes for medium rare to medium doneness; turn occasionally.

3 Carve steaks into slices. Season with salt, as desired. Serve in tortillas with toppings, if desired.

Makes 6 servings (serving size: 2 tacos).

Cook's Note

Tortillas vary in size from very small (about 4 inches in diameter) to large (about 12 inches in diameter). Check your recipe carefully to determine what size to purchase.

★ *Large tortillas are 11 to 12 inches in diameter.*

★ *Medium tortillas are 8 to 10 inches in diameter.*

★ *Small tortillas are 6 to 7 inches in diameter.*

Nutrition Information

Recipe (information per portion size)		page	calories	protein (g)	carbohydrate (g)	fat (g)	iron (mg)	sodium (mg)	cholesterol (mg)
Kitchen Express									
Pesto Beef Sandwich-In-The-Round	⅛ of recipe	23	338	22	35	12	3.3	1307	50
Beef & Broccoli Slaw Wraps	1 wrap	25	498	30	47	20	5.0	1664	81
Beef Soup Provençal	approx. 1½ cups	27	378	32	23	18	6.1	927	74
Beef & Mushroom-Topped Potato Wedges	¼ of recipe	28	422	32	31	21	4.3	858	95
Ginger Beef & Noodle Soup	approx. 1½ cups	29	310	26	11	18	2.8	985	81
Stir-Fried Steak & Vegetable Sandwiches	1 sandwich	30	584	41	58	20	5.7	1131	91
15-Minute Pot Roast With Savory Potatoes	¼ of recipe	31			See ★on page 139.				
Stir-Fried Beef Gyros In Pita Pockets	2 halves	33	558	31	42	29	4.7	797	76
Gorgonzola-Topped Tenderloin Steaks	¼ of recipe	35	308	40	1	15	4.8	278	113
Hurry-Up Beef & Mixed Vegetable Supper	¼ of recipe	37	339	31	24	14	4.1	988	96
Beef Pinwheels With Cucumber & Olives	2 halves	38	485	26	37	27	4.7	1738	96
Ranchero Beef & Rice Skillet	¼ of recipe	39	416	25	41	17	4.4	489	74
Steak, Pear & Walnut Salad	¼ of recipe	41	344	28	15	20	3.4	631	70
Easy Family Meals									
Beef Stir-Fry With Green Beans & Noodles	¼ of recipe	43	486	34	43	20	4.5	1322	71
Ranch Burgers	1 sandwich	45	557	36	24	34	5.1	849	136
Mediterranean Beef Pot Roast & Vegetables	⅙ of recipe	46	453	56	21	14	6.9	497	163
Orange-Glazed Short Ribs With Rice & Peas	¼ of recipe	47	630	62	55	16	9.3	946	172
Easy Steak Milanese	¼ of recipe	49	320	31	15	15	3.7	921	129
Southwest Beef & Chile Pizza	1 wedge	50	386	25	32	17	2.9	849	64
Moroccan Beef Kabobs	1 kabob	51	367	33	26	14	4.5	363	83

Recipe (information per portion size)		page	calories	protein (g)	carbohydrate (g)	fat (g)	iron (mg)	sodium (mg)	cholesterol (mg)
Fresh Tomato, Beef & Bow Tie Pasta	¼ of recipe	53	420	29	35	18	3.9	596	77
Grecian Steak Salad	¼ of recipe	55	401	31	9	27	3.5	574	80
Easy "Meatballs," Vegetables & Pasta	¼ of recipe	56	582	35	63	20	5.4	912	122
Beef & Mushroom Risotto	¼ of recipe	57	434	26	34	20	2.9	971	81
Tasty Taiwan-Ease Beef Salad	¼ of recipe	58	451	32	14	30	4.0	849	76
Sloppy Joe Biscuit Cups	1 biscuit cup	59	265	14	17	16	1.8	635	43
Thai-Style Steak Pizza	1 wedge	61	266	23	18	11	2.7	429	53

Sunday Suppers

Recipe (information per portion size)		page	calories	protein (g)	carbohydrate (g)	fat (g)	iron (mg)	sodium (mg)	cholesterol (mg)
Three-Mushroom Meatloaf	⅙ of recipe	63	323	26	10	20	3.1	817	109
Shredded Beef & Chorizo Sausage Hash	⅙ of recipe	65	274	19	13	16	2.6	480	60
Braised Beef With Mushrooms & Barley	⅛ of recipe	67	293	31	15	12	4.5	498	91
Meatball & Veggie Sandwiches	1 sandwich	68	535	32	46	24	4.3	1029	126
Bold & Beefy Black Bean Chili	approx. 1 cup	69	365	34	24	14	5.6	823	88
Beef & Couscous Stuffed Roasted Peppers	2 halves	71	479	32	44	21	3.8	892	87
Beef & Winter Vegetable Stew	approx. 1½ cups	73	347	29	25	13	3.6	497	73
Savory Beef Empanadas	1 empanada	74	861	31	58	54	5.1	949	112
Pickled Red Onions	approx. ⅓ cup	74	63	0	16	0	0.6	298	0
Hungarian Round Steak & Spaetzle	⅙ of recipe	75	507	44	35	21	5.8	492	142
Beef Enchiladas	2 enchiladas	77	516	30	40	27	5.6	1162	90
Easy Beef Cassoulet	approx. 2 cups	78	384	35	32	12	6.6	878	76
Puff Pastry-Topped Beef Pot Pie	1 pot pie	79	597	36	45	32	5.7	768	78
Corned Beef, Broccoli & Swiss Cheese Pockets	1 pocket	80	482	26	37	26	3.3	1493	91

Nutrition Information

Recipe (information per portion size)		page	calories	protein (g)	carbohydrate (g)	fat (g)	iron (mg)	sodium (mg)	cholesterol (mg)
Cook Once, Dine Twice									
Tex-Mex Beef Wraps With Tomato-Corn Salsa	1 wrap	83	491	45	49	13	4.4	1749	107
Honey-Mustard BBQ Beefwiches	1 sandwich	83	492	44	43	15	5.6	1701	125
10-Minute Beefy Chili	approx. 1 ⅔ cups	85	328	33	27	9	5.1	1621	73
Easy Beef, Vegetable & Tortellini Soup	approx. 2 ¼ cups	85	405	39	36	11	5.6	1673	86
Favorite Family Meatloaf	2 slices	86	274	23	6	17	2.3	469	94
Southern BBQ Meatloaf Sandwiches	1 sandwich	87	445	27	34	22	3.8	973	98
Chili-Salsa Pot Roast	¼ of recipe	88	291	38	7	12	4.8	331	115
Beef & Spanish Rice Taco Salad	¼ of recipe	89	640	41	48	32	5.5	1089	116
Company's Coming									
Beef Kabobs With Asian Noodles	¼ of recipe	91	404	32	32	15	4.6	871	76
Braised Beef	⅙ of recipe	92	282	39	4	11	4.6	495	115
Roasted Vegetables	⅙ of recipe	93	170	3	31	5	3.1	225	0
Mexican Beef Stew	approx. 1 cup	95	383	42	19	15	5.4	479	112
Herb-Crusted Beef Rib Roast	⅛ of recipe	96	453	45	4	28	5.7	146	143
Horseradish-Stuffed Potatoes	1 potato	97	348	6	59	10	3.2	388	25
Four-Pepper Beef Tenderloin	⅙ of recipe	99	257	32	0	13	4.8	460	94
Beef Brisket With Horseradish Sauce	⅙ of recipe	100	385	50	4	18	4.6	200	148
Savory Carrots & Prunes	⅙ of recipe	100	159	2	38	0	1.5	182	0
Quick Beef Burgundy	¼ of recipe	101	*See ★ on page 139.*						
Crumb-Crusted Dijon Sirloin	⅙ of recipe	103	424	35	40	13	5.9	417	93

Recipe (information per portion size)		page	calories	protein (g)	carbohydrate (g)	fat (g)	iron (mg)	sodium (mg)	cholesterol (mg)
Grilled Beef & Smoked Gouda Pizzas	1 pizza	105	745	48	78	28	7.4	1833	108
Beef & Wild Mushroom Lasagna	1/9 of recipe	107	533	34	36	28	3.8	961	106
Curry Beef Stir-Fry With Sugar Snap Peas	1/4 of recipe	109	426	34	31	18	6.1	360	77

Hot Off The Grill

Pacific Rim-Glazed Steak	1/6 of recipe	111	284	24	23	10	2.4	831	57
Grilled Steak & Colorful Peppers	1/4 of recipe	113	336	31	4	22	3.9	76	85
Star-Spangled Cheeseburgers (BBQ Ketchup)	1 sandwich	115	455	30	27	25	3.3	855	97
Star-Spangled Cheeseburgers (Honey Mustard)	1 sandwich	115	485	30	29	27	3.3	876	99
Spicy Ribeyes With Grilled Sweet Onions	1/4 of recipe	117	430	38	19	22	4.1	680	102
Sizzling Summer Steak	1/6 of recipe	119	239	36	1	9	3.3	167	95
Grilled Steaks With Tomato & Pesto Pasta	1/4 of recipe	120	640	53	37	30	6.3	172	124
Balsamic-Marinated Sirloin & Asparagus	1/4 of recipe	121	214	27	4	10	3.5	373	76
Rosemary-Pepper Beef With Steak Fries	1/4 of recipe	123	492	48	23	22	4.2	290	121
Grilled Garlic-Stuffed Steaks	1/6 of recipe	125	239	33	3	10	3.8	170	95
Citrus-Ginger Beef Teriyaki	1/4 of recipe	127	377	33	20	18	4.3	1899	101
Italian-Stuffed Burgers	1 sandwich	128	536	40	28	29	5.2	723	120
Grilled Beef Quesadillas	2 quesadillas	129	799	48	66	36	5.8	1941	122
Steak Salad With Ranch Dressing	1/4 of recipe	131	323	28	6	21	4.3	484	86
Island Jerk Beef & Pineapple Kabobs	1/4 of recipe	132	397	31	27	19	5.3	866	117
Grilled Steak Santa Fe	1/4 of recipe	133	333	29	14	18	4.2	208	71
Steak Soft Tacos	2 tacos	135	418	30	35	17	5.0	495	75

★ *Due to the variations among fully cooked, ready-to-heat-and-eat boneless pot roast brands, nutrition information could not be calculated. See package for additional information.*

Index